I0006624

MANAGING YOUR OUTSOURCED IT SERVICES PROVIDER

HOW TO UNLEASH THE FULL POTENTIAL OF YOUR GLOBAL WORKFORCE

Venkatesh Upadrista

Apress®

Managing Your Outsourced IT Services Provider: How to Unleash the Full Potential of Your Global Workforce

Copyright © 2015 by **Venkatesh Upadrista**

This work is subject to copyright. All rights are reserved by the Publisher, whether the whole or part of the material is concerned, specifically the rights of translation, reprinting, reuse of illustrations, recitation, broadcasting, reproduction on microfilms or in any other physical way, and transmission or information storage and retrieval, electronic adaptation, computer software, or by similar or dissimilar methodology now known or hereafter developed. Exempted from this legal reservation are brief excerpts in connection with reviews or scholarly analysis or material supplied specifically for the purpose of being entered and executed on a computer system, for exclusive use by the purchaser of the work. Duplication of this publication or parts thereof is permitted only under the provisions of the Copyright Law of the Publisher's location, in its current version, and permission for use must always be obtained from Springer. Permissions for use may be obtained through RightsLink at the Copyright Clearance Center. Violations are liable to prosecution under the respective Copyright Law.

ISBN-13 (pbk): 978-1-4842-0803-8

ISBN-13 (electronic): 978-1-4842-0802-1

Trademarked names, logos, and images may appear in this book. Rather than use a trademark symbol with every occurrence of a trademarked name, logo, or image we use the names, logos, and images only in an editorial fashion and to the benefit of the trademark owner, with no intention of infringement of the trademark.

The use in this publication of trade names, trademarks, service marks, and similar terms, even if they are not identified as such, is not to be taken as an expression of opinion as to whether or not they are subject to proprietary rights.

While the advice and information in this book are believed to be true and accurate at the date of publication, neither the authors nor the editors nor the publisher can accept any legal responsibility for any errors or omissions that may be made. The publisher makes no warranty, express or implied, with respect to the material contained herein.

Managing Director: Welmoed Spahr
Acquisitions Editor: Robert Hutchinson
Developmental Editor: James Markham
Editorial Board: Steve Anglin, Mark Beckner, Gary Cornell, Louise Corrigan, James DeWolf,
    Jonathan Gennick, Robert Hutchinson, Michelle Lowman, James Markham,
    Matthew Moodie, Jeff Olson, Jeffrey Pepper, Douglas Pundick, Ben Renow-Clarke,
    Gwenan Spearing, Matt Wade, Steve Weiss
Coordinating Editor: Rita Fernando
Copy Editor: Tiffany Taylor
Compositor: SPi Global
Indexer: SPi Global

Distributed to the book trade worldwide by Springer Science+Business Media New York, 233 Spring Street, 6th Floor, New York, NY 10013. Phone 1-800-SPRINGER, fax (201) 348-4505, e-mail orders-ny@springer-sbm.com, or visit www.springeronline.com. Apress Media, LLC is a California LLC and the sole member (owner) is Springer Science + Business Media Finance Inc (SSBM Finance Inc). SSBM Finance Inc is a Delaware corporation.

For information on translations, please e-mail rights@apress.com, or visit www.apress.com.

Apress and friends of ED books may be purchased in bulk for academic, corporate, or promotional use. eBook versions and licenses are also available for most titles. For more information, reference our Special Bulk Sales–eBook Licensing web page at www.apress.com/bulk-sales.

Any source code or other supplementary materials referenced by the author in this text is available to readers at www.apress.com. For detailed information about how to locate your book's source code, go to www.apress.com/source-code/.

Apress Business: The Unbiased Source of Business Information

Apress business books provide essential information and practical advice, each written for practitioners by recognized experts. Busy managers and professionals in all areas of the business world—and at all levels of technical sophistication—look to our books for the actionable ideas and tools they need to solve problems, update and enhance their professional skills, make their work lives easier, and capitalize on opportunity.

Whatever the topic on the business spectrum—entrepreneurship, finance, sales, marketing, management, regulation, information technology, among others—Apress has been praised for providing the objective information and unbiased advice you need to excel in your daily work life. Our authors have no axes to grind; they understand they have one job only—to deliver up-to-date, accurate information simply, concisely, and with deep insight that addresses the real needs of our readers.

It is increasingly hard to find information—whether in the news media, on the Internet, and now all too often in books—that is even-handed and has your best interests at heart. We therefore hope that you enjoy this book, which has been carefully crafted to meet our standards of quality and unbiased coverage.

We are always interested in your feedback or ideas for new titles. Perhaps you'd even like to write a book yourself. Whatever the case, reach out to us at editorial@apress.com and an editor will respond swiftly. Incidentally, at the back of this book, you will find a list of useful related titles. Please visit us at www.apress.com to sign up for newsletters and discounts on future purchases.

The Apress Business Team

Contents

About the Author

Venkatesh Upadrista currently works for a large services company where he holds responsibility at the business-unit level for managing multiple large client relationships. During his IT career, he has won several large business deals based on his knowledge of consultative selling techniques and IT outsourcing.

Venkatesh began compiling management encyclopedias as a high school student nearly 25 years ago. He has taken a vast collection of experimental facts from various sources and the research he has accumulated over the years and deployed them throughout his professional experience.

He is an advisor to a number of business-development initiatives and has been a partner to the CIOs of several large organizations, helping them define ways to improve their top line and bottom line and to prioritize their IT outsourcing business initiatives.

Venkatesh's experience encompasses project management, sales leadership, and IT outsourcing. He has worked in a blended mixture of the onsite/offshore model and, through his experience, has helped many customers shift their strategies to gain qualitative and quantitative benefits.

Acknowledgments

I have had the opportunity to interact with several CIOs over the last two decades of my experience in the information technology (IT) industry. I have consulted with several C-level executives on IT outsourcing and worked with IT services companies ranging from small to billion-dollar multinational companies in various roles. During my experience, almost all of my customers had a similar concern: they were unable to extract the full value from their service providers. In contrast, however, they did receive what had been agreed on in the contract. Some were worried that they might be locked in with their vendor services.

This book is, in a way, an outcome of my experience with customers that outsourced their IT business to service providers. The successes and failures I've heard about and experienced in IT outsourcing and the extensive research and experiments I have carried out have a common thread: due to lack of understanding of their IT service providers' organizational structure, goals, and objectives, organizations were unable to get maximum results from those service providers. Personally, I have seen enormous success in IT outsourcing, which was the inspiration for me to craft this book. I thank all of those people who have worked with me to achieve the common goal of bringing these efforts to fruition.

I am grateful to all the employers with whom I have worked. They have given me the rich experience that underlies this project. I am thankful to my sponsoring editor from Apress for providing me with important advice on formatting the book and managing the project smoothly. I also appreciate the efforts of the editing team for giving my flow and expressions a facelift and guiding me through the manuscript development process.

Most important, I would like to thank my guide, Siva, for helping me to complete this project. I hope his blessings are always with me throughout my life. My special thanks to my family for supporting me in this project—for giving up so many weekends, for tolerating the late nights required to put this together, and for cheering me along through every step of writing this book.

Introduction

Organizations seek to focus on their core business processes while delegating noncore processes; they consequently select a service provider to manage these noncore tasks. In the information technology (IT) services industry, a business that provides services is referred to as a *service provider organization (SPO)*, and the receiver of such services is called a *service receiver organization (SRO)*. In such a scenario, personnel from the SRO become customers of the SPO.

Over the past several decades, IT outsourcing has become increasingly common; many organizations find that they are able to reduce their costs and focus on their core business processes when IT outsourcing is adopted. However, a common concern expressed by executives from many IT SROs is that even though they partner with well-established IT SPOs, they are unable to extract the full potential of those SPOs. In my discussions with several such executives, they have consistently reported that the SPO is not sufficiently proactive or innovative to bring added value to its customers.

Although this topic is debatable, the essential point is that the SRO should ideally be able to follow an approach that will help it to obtain maximum benefits from its SPOs. This book explains the key concepts related to this topic and adopts the mantra, "Understand your service provider to manage your service provider." But to succeed in this journey, it is essential that SRO fully support the SPO to achieve the expectations.

This book is divided into two sections. The first section discusses the classification of different types of IT SPOs based on their size and location, how these companies are organized, their strengths and weaknesses, and their goals and objectives. This section also provides information about the financial targets of IT SPOs and the strategies that such organizations typically adopt in order to achieve these targets. Reading this section, you will be able to comprehensively understand IT SPOs, with the objective of using this information to manage your SPOs in a more efficient manner.

After establishing the basics of SPOs, the second part of this book explains in detail how to manage your SPOs. It explains various concepts you need to address when establishing a relationship with an SPO, what to expect (and what not to expect) from an SPO, how to utilize its strengths and mitigate risks related to its weaknesses, and how to use this information to secure the best service available. Using several case studies and examples, this section explains how to do the following:

- Engage and manage SPO staff
- Define financial targets to achieve the best value for your money
- Extract full value from each staff member of the SPO
- Define contracts that can provide long-term benefits
- Understand potential pitfalls in contracts with SPOs and how to manage these challenges
- Manage vendor lock-in: a situation in which an SRO becomes fully dependent on an SPO product or service and does not possess the required knowledge to perform the work in-house or transition to another SPO

This part of the book also discusses single-provider sourcing strategies, including the advantages and drawbacks of such arrangements. The salient topics for organizations motivated to enter into a single-sourcing model are addressed. Further, this section discusses the evolution of captive units, including how captives should be empowered and structured by organizations to enable them to deliver optimal results. A captive unit, in an IT outsourcing context, is a business unit of a company functioning offshore as an entity of its own, managing part or all of the company's IT needs with close operational ties to the parent company.

Although the concepts presented can be applied to any industry, this book has been written with a focus on IT. It is targeted to all individuals who outsource their IT business to a service provider.

Reading this book, individuals from SROs will learn how to better understand their SPOs and will gain skills in managing them in order to gain the maximum value for the benefit of the SRO.

Understanding the Outsourced IT Service Provider Industry

Part I of this book is designed to help you understand the basics of the IT services industry and to explain the different types of IT service companies in the market today. It includes an explanation of the goals and objectives of IT service provider organizations (SPOs) in addition to providing a detailed overview of how a typical IT SPO is organized, the different roles in the organization, and those roles' responsibilities. This part also explains the SPO's profit-and-loss parameters, its strengths and weaknesses regarding its financial targets, and what organizations typically do to achieve their targets.

After reading this section, you will have a general understanding of IT SPOs and will be able to use this information to manage your own SPO in a more efficient manner

The Organization of IT Service Providers

A service industry provides services to aid its client companies in achieving their business objectives. An organization that intends to continue focusing on its core business processes while delegating noncore processes selects a service provider. The expectation in the business environment is that every organization should be innovative in its core business processes to achieve frontrunner status in its industry.

Definitions An *organization*, in the context of this book, is a company that performs business in any industry such as manufacturing, retail, banking, insurance, aerospace, or information technology.

A *service provider* or a *service provider organization* is a is a company that provides other organizations with consulting, software, hardware, legal, real estate, education, communications, and many other types of services based on each service receiver organization's core area of business. In some instances, the concept of *service provider* refers to organizational subunits, but—in more general terms and throughout this book—the term *service provider* refers to a third-party or outsourced supplier.

An **IT service provider** or an **IT service provider organization (SPO)** is a company that provides other organizations with information technology (IT). Organizations that receive IT services (from IT service providers) are called **IT service receivers** or **IT service receiver organizations (SROs)**.

There are different types of service organizations; the IT industry is one type. Worldwide IT spending is projected to total $3.8 trillion in 2014.[1] This suggests the pace at which the IT industry is expanding, and IT service companies are taking full advantage of this growth.

In the IT industry, personnel from the SRO become customers of the SPO. The SPO is also often referred to as a vendor of the SRO.

Classification of IT Service Organizations

Broadly speaking, there are two types of IT **SPOs,** depending on the location of their headquarters. As detailed in the next two sections, *multinational companies* (MNCs) have their headquarters in developed countries (defined **next**), whereas *pure players* have their headquarters in *developing countries* (defined **next**).

▓ **Definitions**   A developed country, in the context of IT outsourcing, is a country where the cost of performing IT services is high relative to other countries. This is because a developed country has a high cost of living, a developed industrial base, and a high human-development index relative to other countries, which translates to a high cost for IT services. Some examples of developed countries are the United States, the United Kingdom, Canada, France, Australia, and Spain.

A developing country, in the context of IT outsourcing, is a country where the cost of performing IT services is low relative to developed countries. This is because a developing country has a low cost of living, a developing industrial base, and a low human-development index relative to developed countries, which translates to a low cost for IT services. Some examples of developing countries are India, China, Thailand, and the Philippines.

IT **SPOs** are alternatively classified as *Tier-1, Tier-2,* or *Tier-3* IT service providers, based on their year-on-year revenue and employee strength, as detailed in the appropriately headed sections.

---

[1]Gartner, "Gartner Says Worldwide IT Spending on Pace to Reach $3.8 Trillion in 2014", *Gartner Newsroom,* January 6, 2012, www.gartner.com/newsroom/id/2643919.

Multinational IT Service Providers

Multinational IT service providers are MNCs that have their headquarters in developed countries, with development centers and sales offices across the world in both developed and developing countries. IBM, Accenture, and Capgemini exemplify multinational IT service providers. Typically, in this type of organization, more than 60% of the company staff operates from developed countries. With changing market conditions and pressures on cost, some of these organizations have started to adopt a long-term goal of increasing their staff in developing countries. Table 1-1 shows a 2013 estimate of the sizes of the workforces of several MNCs in a developing country—in this instance, India—as fractions of their global workforces.

Table 1-1. Employee Figures for Several MNCs in India (2013)[2]

MNC	Base Location	Total Number of Employees	Total Number of Employees in India	Percentage of Employees in India
Capgemini	France	125,000	44,000	35%
Accenture	United States	275,000	>90,000	33%
CSC	United States	98,000	24,000	25%
IBM	United States	430,000	130,000	30%

Pure-Play IT Service Providers

Pure-play service providers—or simply *pure players*—have their headquarters in developing countries such as India, China, and the Philippines. With their headquarters and a large portion of their workforce deployed in developing countries, pure players conduct business with clients across the world in both developed and developing countries. Table 1-2 shows the sizes of the workforces of several pure players in a developing country—in this instance, India or China—all of which fall well above the threshold rule that 60% of a company's global workforce be in the base developing country for that company to be considered a pure player.

---

[2]Shilpa Phadnis and Sujit John, "Top Global IT Firms Have More Staff in India Than Home Nations," *Times of India*, November 6, 2013, http://timesofindia.indiatimes. com/tech/jobs/Top-global-IT-firms-have-more-staff-in-India-than-home-nations/articleshow/25280494.cms.

Table 1-2. Employee Figures for Pure Players (2013 and 2014)

Company	Base Country	Total Number of Employees	Total Number of Employees in Base Country	Percentage of Employees in Base Country
Infosys[3]	India	160,405	123,847	77.2%
Hexaware[4]	India	8,854	6,835	77%
Neusoft[5]	China	22,403	21,712	97%

Tier-1 IT Service Providers

Organizations with revenues of more than US $1 billion and having an employee base of more than 50,000 are categorized as Tier-1 IT service providers. From their strengths in legacy application development and application maintenance, these organizations invest to provide end-to-end software services spanning consulting, *business process outsourcing* (BPO), and IT infrastructure services.

Tier-1 IT service providers are further classified as *Tier-1 MNC* or *Tier-1 pure player*, based on the location of their headquarters and predominant geographical presence. Typically, these types of organizations have offices in most countries across the world and service their customers with a global delivery model.

Tier-2 IT Service Providers

Tier-2 IT service providers are organizations with revenues less than US $1 billion and employees numbering between 10,000 and 50,000. This type of organization specializes in and services clients of specific industries such as banking and financial services, aerospace, retail, and manufacturing, with a focus on specific geographies. Within these verticals and geographies, these organizations compete with Tier-1 service providers.

Tier-2 IT service providers are further classified as *Tier-2 MNCs* or *Tier-2 pure players*, based on the location of their headquarters and predominant geographical presence.

---

[3]Infosys Ltd. Form 20-F (p. 16), US SEC, May 9, 2014, www.infosys.com/investors/reports-filings/annual-report/form20f/Documents/form20F-2014.pdf.
[4]Hexaware Technologies Ltd. 2013 Annual Report, http://hexaware.com/fileadd/Hexaware-Annual-Report-2013.pdf.
[5]Neusoft Corporation 2013 Annual Report, www.neusoft.com/upload/files/20140716/1405493519488.pdf.

Tier-3 IT Service Providers

These companies have revenues less than US $100 million and an employee base of fewer than 1,000. These organizations focus on very niche and narrow services, with a focus on limited geographies, and they aim to provide end-to-end services within these services and geographies.

The Corporate Organization of an IT Service Provider

Although each organization has a unique method of managing its operations and business, at a broader level, almost all IT SPOs structure themselves in a similar fashion. Every organization consists of three broad pillars: industry verticals or business units, service lines or practices, and support functions (Figure 1-1).

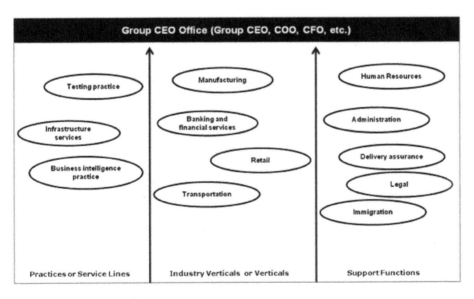

Figure 1-1. Organizational structure of an IT SPO, with three core pillars

Verticals

A *vertical* is an entity within an SPO that specializes in selling and delivering services to clients belonging to a specific industry or domain, such as the banking industry, financial services industry, or manufacturing industry. In some organizations, verticals are also referred to as *business units* or *strategic business units.* Staff in a vertical are experienced and knowledgeable about their respective domain and services. Examples of verticals include the following:

- *Banking and financial services vertical*—Services all banks and financial institutions. IT needs are serviced by this vertical across geographies for retail banks, investment banks, and credit card companies, among other clients.

- *Insurance vertical*—Services the IT needs of all types of insurance companies, including life insurance, auto insurance, travel insurance, and so on.

Typically, personnel from verticals hold profit-and-loss accountability. The profitability and revenue achievements of a particular vertical are measured in relation to three targets: the top line, the bottom line, and utilization of resources.

Definitions The *top line* is a company's gross sales or revenues. In other words, it indicates the total money that is being paid by customers to a service provider. Therefore, a company's *top-line growth* refers to an increase in gross sales or revenues.

The *bottom line* is the net income on a company's income statement. This is the income after all expenses such as salaries, interest charges, taxes, and general and administrative costs have been deducted from revenues. The bottom line is also referred as the *profit margin*.

The *utilization* or *utilization rate* of an individual is the billing efficiency of that individual. In other words, it indicates the labor cost of an individual that is paid by the client.

The utilization rate is calculated as the number of billable hours divided by the number of working hours recorded over a particular time period by an individual. For example, say an employee was in the office 30 hours last week, but only 20 of those hours were paid for by the customer. In this case, the utilization rate for this employee is $20 \div 30 = 66\%$.

The utilization rate of a practice, a vertical, or an organization is calculated as the sum of all billable employee hours of each employee within a practice, a vertical, or an organization divided by the total number of working hours recorded by all those employees in a particular period. For example, say a practice has 100 employees out of which 90 employees were in the office and paid by customer for the complete month. In this case, the utilization rate for this practice is $90 \div 100 = 90\%$.

Practices

A *practice* is an entity within an SPO that specializes in selling and delivering services that address a specific technology or domain. Such technologies or domains are also referred to as *subject matter areas*. In contrast to a vertical, which services customers belonging to a specific industry or domain, a practice serves customers in a *horizontal* across several or all verticals (discussed in the "Practice Structure" section). Practices closely liaise with verticals to understand customer needs, and they bring their services to customers by collaborating with verticals. Two examples of practice subject-matter areas follow:

- *Testing practice*—Provides automation and manual testing services for customers across manufacturing, banking and financial services, and retail.

- *Business intelligence (BI) practice*—Provides an end-to-end suite of BI services to assist customers with devising business insights to enhance decision-making and financial management. Organizational offerings range from devising BI strategies to implementing best-fit tools and solutions, including creating dashboards and scorecards. These organizations service clients across verticals and work hand-in-hand with vertical teams to sell and deliver to service clients.

Typical practices have top-line and utilization targets in their area of business, in addition to the objective of establishing new services within the domain. Top-line targets indicate that they must retain business in their existing client base and increase business by acquiring new clients. However, they are mandated to liaise with teams from verticals in order to achieve business development.

Most organizations create an entity within each practice horizontal called a *center of excellence*—a group or department that focuses on specific areas looking both inside and outside the organization to capture new knowledge and practices. In addition, this group is responsible for developing tools and techniques within the purview of the horizontal subject-matter area that can bring value to the customer. Within their testing practice, for example, most organizations create an automation-tools group whose main goal is to develop custom tools and interfaces that can enhance automation over and above the tools available in the market. These tools are the intellectual property of the SPO.

Support Functions

A *support function* is an entity within an organization that stands as a pillar in support of overall organizational structures, such as verticals and practices. Verticals and practices are considered to be the core functions of any IT SPO, whereas support functions are non-core and serve to facilitate the core operations of the business. Support functions include finance, human resources (HR), legal, and administration. Support functions do not directly interact with customers.

The Governance of an IT SPO

The governance of any particular organization is structured in strict accordance with the particular strategy the organization employs. At a broader level, however, all IT SPOs have similar forms of governance. Figure 1-2 depicts the typical organizational governance followed by most IT SPOs.

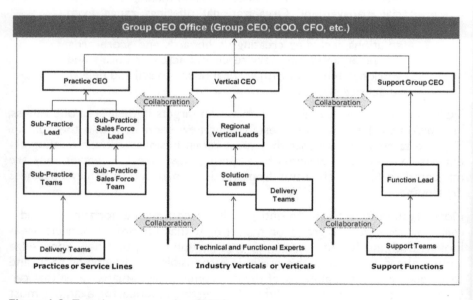

Figure 1-2. Typical governance of an IT SPO

Each organization starts with the group chief executive officer (CEO): the head of the organization, who reports to the board of directors and the chairperson or founder of the company. One level down, all entities of the organization reporting to the group CEO, such as the verticals, practices, and support functions. Each vertical and practice of an organization has a CEO whose core function is to ensure that the CEO's business is profitable and growing at a fast pace, with targets related to top-line and bottom-line growth. The CEO must also ensure that assets are created within the organization that differentiate the vertical or practice from peer organizations.

The CEO of the support function reports to the group CEO and is accountable for ensuring that the support group is providing support to the verticals and practices adequate to permit them to perform their jobs efficiently and effectively. As an example, HR management is a support function, and one of the responsibilities of this function is to ensure that the proper set of resources is employed at the correct time, based on the resource needs of the verticals and practices. Another example of a support function is the administration group, which must ensure that proper physical space is provided for resources belonging to the verticals and practices to run the business efficiently and effectively.

Vertical Structure

A typical example of a vertical organizational structure is depicted in Figure 1-3. A vertical has accountability for profit and loss in its respective area of business.

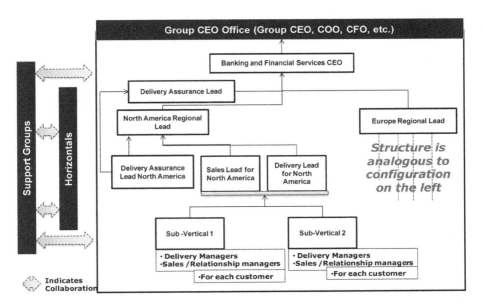

Figure 1-3. Vertical organizational structure and its collaboration with different support groups and horizontals

Figure 1-3 indicates that each vertical of an IT SPO is helmed by a vertical CEO to whom all regional leads report, based on the geography in which the vertical has a business presence. Within each of these geographies, there is a division between delivery leaders and sales leaders, who have respective delivery and sales responsibilities to achieve in the region.

A *delivery assurance group* is an independent group within an SPO, responsible for advising, supporting, and reviewing projects and programmers on all aspects of the solution delivery lifecycle. This group collects and manages best practices and metrics, defines quality guidelines to be followed in projects, selects usage of tools and procedures, and coordinates institutionalizing and tracking all these aspects while teams are delivering projects.

There may be several verticals within an SPO, based on their area of business, and each such vertical features a similar structure.

Practice Structure

As explained earlier, a *practice*—also referred to as a *service line* or *horizontal*—is a technical entity within an SPO that provides specific technical and domain capabilities in specific areas of work. Unlike a vertical structure, which is specific to an industry, a horizontal is not limited to a vertical industry; rather, it services all customers across verticals in an SPO.

Figure 1-4 provides an example of a practice structure that is commonly followed across most SPOs.

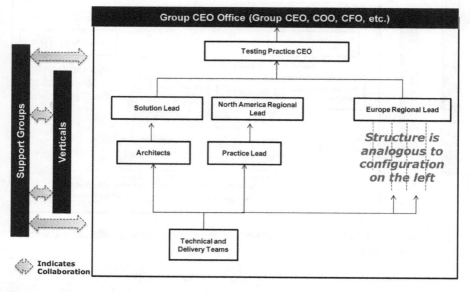

Figure 1-4. Example of a practice structure

Like a vertical structure, a practice structure has a CEO at the helm, whose core responsibilities are top-line business growth, utilization of resources within the practice, and establishing solutions. This *practice CEO* has geographic leaders to manage business in the respective regions. In addition, the practice CEO typically has a *solution lead* whose responsibility is to ensure that existing solutions are enhanced based on market demands. The practice CEO must establish new services that can differentiate the company from its peer organizations in each subject matter of this practice. These services are further utilized by the regional-level *practice leads* and their teams tasked with selling to customers.

Practice leads are accountable to sell practice services within their geographical region to their client base. During this process, practice leads coordinate with vertical teams to sell services. Practice leads are responsible for managing the top line within their geographical region.

Support Group Structure

As stated previously, a *support group* is an entity within an SPO that provides support to verticals and practices that are necessary in order for them to conduct their business effectively. Figure 1-5 depicts a typical example of support group governance in an SPO. This entity is governed by the support group CEO.

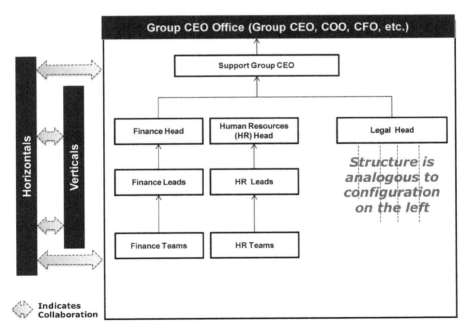

Figure 1-5. Example of a support group structure

A support group serves several functions, a few of which are listed next. Each function is led by a *function head* who oversees teams based on the size of the business being handled:

- *Human resources*: Broadly speaking, the key responsibilities of an HR department encompass numerous functions including human resource planning, determining wages and salaries of employees, recruitment and selection, performance appraisals, training and development, employee welfare and motivation, and implementing human resource policies. HR practitioners in each discipline may perform more than one function. In small businesses without a dedicated HR department, it is still possible to achieve the same level of efficiency and workforce management as in larger organizations. However, in mid- to large-sized organizations, a separate HR function is established.

- *Legal*: Over the course of conducting a company's daily functions, many legal issues become apparent, which require qualified advice from lawyers and legal advisors. Legal support involves providing advice in such matters as resolving contractual issues or breaches, representing company conflicts in the courts, intellectual property infringement, copyright issues, and breaches of data privacy.

- *Finance*: Finance is another key department for any IT SPO that manages money transactions. The business functions of a finance department typically include planning, organizing, auditing, accounting for, and controlling its company's finances. The finance department also typically produces the company's financial statements and closely integrates with the verticals and practices during any business transactions in addition to closely monitoring and controlling the financials of projects during project execution. Typically, the finance department reports to the chief financial officer (CFO) of the SPO.

Case Study of Cooperation among Entities in an SPO

The preceding sections discussed the different entities of an IT SPO in conceptual isolation from each other. The following hypothetical case study illustrates how different entities in an SPO cooperate to service their common customer.

> *SPO profile: Company A, a leading Tier-1 pure player headquartered in India*
>
> *Size: 120,000 employees*
>
> *Client profile of Company A: XYZ Financials, a leading organization specializing in the credit card business*
>
> *Size: 90,000 employees*

The story begins in early 2YYY. In this year, XYZ Financials has a market capitalization of $50 billion and an IT budget of $200 million per year. For decades, the organization has been doing most of its work in-house. After coming to understand the merits of IT outsourcing, it contacted a leading consulting company to provide advice on how to engage an IT service provider. After extensively analyzing the IT landscape and assessing the strengths and weaknesses of XYZ Financials, the consulting company provided a list of five IT service providers and asked XYZ Financials to contact these providers for the purpose of outsourcing the company's IT services.

In those days, I was working with one of the leading pure players, Company A, and we were among the five IT service providers to be contacted. At a high level, the request for a business proposal was intended to enhance the existing credit-processing applications of XYZ Financials with new features and to provide maintenance and support for these applications. These applications were hosted using a mix of mainframe, Java, and .NET technologies. The goal was to achieve a faster time to market, and service providers were asked to adopt an agile development methodology.

We assessed the details of the request made by XYZ Financials. I was a member of the payments sub-vertical, which was part of the financial services vertical of Company A, and I was asked to help respond to this business request. Figure 1-6 shows the employees in my organization who were involved in responding to the XYZ Financials proposal.

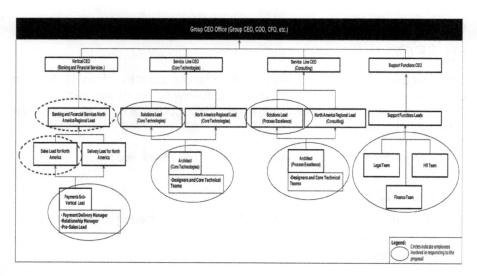

Figure 1-6. Employee structure of Company A

Because this proposal was related to a customer in the payment domain, it was managed by the payments sub-vertical of the banking department and the financial services vertical of Company A.

Because mainframe, Java, and .NET technology expertise were at that time components of the core technologies service line, we involved this service line as part of the negotiation. Another requirement of this proposal was to adopt agile methodologies in the projects undertaken and to employ a process consulting group of the consulting service line specializing in this area. The process consulting group was therefore involved in this deal.

To respond to the request from XYZ Financials, it was ultimately decided that the banking and financial services vertical would lead this deal with support from the payments sub-vertical, core technologies service line, and process consulting group.

The vertical sales team was responsible for the front end of the customer relationship; accordingly, the banking and financial services North America regional lead and sales lead for North America are marked in dotted lines in Figure 1-5. Together, they were given the responsibility of spearheading the sales and client interaction process for this deal.

The domain solution was to be delivered by the payments sub-vertical, and I was asked to lead this initiative. The technical solution was to be delivered by the core technology service line, based on its past experiences and its process consulting group for agile methodology.

The following support teams were also engaged:

- *Legal team*—To provide legal assessments of the deal

- *HR function*—To ensure that sufficient resources were available to manage the projects once the deal was finalized

- *Finance team*—To validate the financial components of the deal

To gather all participating components together for the deal, a pre-sales lead was appointed from the payments sub-vertical; his job was to collate and integrate the various solutions originating from different teams. The delivery manager from the payments sub-vertical was responsible for ensuring that the overall solution adhered to the needs of XYZ Financials. This structure constituted the entire team and construct for responding to the proposal from XYZ Financials.

Almost all organizations bring together teams in a similar fashion based on the needs and requests of their clients. Based on the size of the deal, appropriate employees from the organization are involved. In multimillion-dollar deals, the CEOs can be involved to manage client relationships and also to review the solution created for the agreement.

Once the contract has been won, the service lines and verticals involved in constructing the agreement are ultimately responsible for delivering the specified projects.

The Strategy Changes, but the Structure Does Not

Organizations that view organizational structure as separate from strategy can never grow beyond a certain limit. Organizations that fail to adapt their structures to evolving market needs and organizational strategies experience losses and they eventually go out of business.

Structures must be continually revised in order to improve efficiency, promote teamwork, create synergy, and reduce costs. As soon as organizations fail to change their structure based on evolving market demands and strategies, they become obsolete.

Structure and strategy are dependent on each other. You can create the most efficient, team-oriented, synergistic structure possible and still end up in the same place you were, or even experience a decline.

Structure is not simply captured as an organizational chart or a reporting hierarchy. It involves people, positions, procedures, processes, culture, technology, and related elements that form the organization. Organizations often fail after they have acquired another company because, even though the strategy behind the acquisition was well reasoned, the structure remained the same after the acquisition, which stifled success.

Each organizational structure must be completely integrated with a strategy for the organization to achieve its mission and goals. Structure supports strategy.

Key Points

- An IT service provider is a company that provides organizations with IT consulting, software, and hardware services.

- An IT service receiver is a company that engages with a service provider to receive IT consulting, software, and hardware services.

- A multinational IT service provider (MNC) is an organization that has its headquarters in a developed country and development centers and sales offices across the world in both developed and developing countries.

- A pure play service provider is an organization that has its headquarters in a developing country and conducts business with clients across the world in both developed and developing countries.

- An organization with revenues of more than US $1 billion and an employee base of more than 50,000 is categorized as a Tier-1 IT service provider.

- An organization with revenues of less than US $1 billion and an employee base between 10,000 and 50,000 is categorized as a Tier-2 IT service provider.

- An organization with revenues of less than US $100 million and an employee base of less than 1,000 is categorized as a Tier-3 IT service provider.

- Every IT SPO consists of three pillars: industry verticals or business units, service lines or practices, and support functions.

- A practice is an entity within a SPO that specializes in selling and delivering services addressing a specific technology or domain.

- A vertical is an entity within a SPO that specializes in selling and delivering services to clients belonging to a specific industry or domain.

- A support function is an entity within an organization that supports overall organizational structures, such as verticals and practices.

The Profit-and-Loss Constraints on IT Services Provider Organizations

Many IT service provider organizations (SPOs) have high expectations for revenue growth, but few manage to sustainably expand their customer base year after year. Many IT SPOs have high expectations to increase their profitability, but very few manage to achieve profits beyond a certain limit.

A few IT SPOs have been able to grow in terms of both revenue and profitability because they have always been able to strike the proper balance between profitability and quality of service, where quality of service has always been their top priority. They followed a strategy that enabled them to continually increase their client base by delivering high-quality services and being profitable. Being profitable is never inversely proportional to quality of service. The core philosophy adopted by every successful IT SPO ensures that their customers receive high-quality products and services and that profits are not prioritized to the extent that the quality of service would be negatively affected. Such IT SPOs have always been the frontrunners.

Today, the global atmosphere favors IT SPOs that have demonstrated specialized skills with respect to introducing new services or products in their organization. Such IT SPOs continually introduce high-technology systems and services that assure them a competitive edge. As a result of heavy competition, and with a view to having a greater market share, these IT SPOs offer the services for which they are best suited instead of trying to experiment with new areas in which they do not have expertise; this way, they do not lose their competitive edge in their area of expertise. But they keep up to date on new technology and processes in order to maintain an advantage over their competitors—no IT SPO, however collaborative, wants to lag behind in state-of-the-art technology or processes.

Processes and technologies do not create a distinction between developed and developing IT SPOs or make an organization unique. By their very nature, processes are beneficial to organizations for socioeconomic development, and the leading organizations try to implement the best of these.

IT SPOs are made up of people. Individuals can only adapt to organizational changes and appreciate the full potential of their organization if that organization provides them with a platform to understand the changes for which an investment is required.

Successful IT SPOs have never compromised on these investments, which means they are investing in understanding market needs and developing themselves and their employees without worrying that these investments do not have a guaranteed return. Other IT SPOs, however, are able to increase their profitability in the short term by not investing in such efforts; they are always at risk of going out of business due to a lack of understanding of market needs.

Every organization, regardless of industry, is considered successful based on business growth, which is defined by revenue and profitability, or *margin*. Two pillars of every IT service organization are continually under supervision: the top line and the bottom line.

The Top Line

The *top line* refers to an IT SPO's gross sales or revenue. (This excludes non-profit organizations, because the annual revenue for such organizations is referred to as *gross receipts* and includes donations, benefits, government support, income from activities related to the organization's mission, and income from fundraising activities.)

As in other industries, revenue is a crucial part of the financial analysis for IT SPOs. Revenue determines the health of the organization. An IT SPO's performance is measured by the extent to which its asset inflows (revenues) compare with its asset outflows (expenses).

All IT SPOs desire top-line growth, because this directly indicates their growth in business and market share. A typical Tier-1 IT SPO posts revenue increases between 20% and 25% year-on-year.

According to the Dataquest annual review of the Indian IT industry, the top 200 IT SPOs in India reported a combined revenue of $84 billion USD in FY 2011. Table 2-1 presents the growth figures of different IT services.

Table 2-1. Dataquest Top 20 IT SPOs in India: FY 2010-2011[1]

Revenue in RS Crore

Rank 09-10	Rank 10-11	Organization	Revenue FY 11	Revenue FY 10	% growth FY '11
1	1	TCS	33,112	26,576	25
3	2	Infosys Technologies	25,997	21,355	22
2	3	Wipro	24,899	21,949	13
4	4	Hewlett-Packard India	23,227	17,831	30
5	5	Cognizant Technology Solutions	21,393	15,646	37
6	6	IBM India	14,132	12,388	14
8	7	HCL Technologies	14,111	10,983	28
7	8	HCL Infosystems	12,137	11,956	2
9	9	Ingram Micro India	9,766	7,234	35
10	10	Redington India	9,274	7,024	32
12	11	Cisco Systems India	8,157	6,057	35
11	12	Oracle India	7,934	6,321	26
13	13	Dell India	7,666	5,709	34
14	14	Intel India	6,108	5,160	18
15	15	Accenture India	5,672	4,800	18
17	16	SAP India	5,146	3,924	31
New	17	Mahindra Satyam	5,049	5,084	-1
16	18	Tech Mahindra	4,819	4,359	11
19	19	Microsoft India	4,711	3,910	20
18	20	Mphasis	4,498	3,920	15

[1]Source: CyberMedia, DataQuest Top 20 IT Companies, July 2011. The DQ Top 20 takes into account revenues of IT companies from April 1, 2010 to March 31, 2011. Although different companies have different financial years, DataQuest has taken April–March revenue for each company to maintain uniformity in comparison. Only the Mphasis revenue period differs: it is assessed from May 1, 2010 to April 30, 2011.

It has been demonstrated across the industry that well-defined, growing Tier-2 or Tier-3 IT SPOs post growth from 20% to as much as 300% year-on-year until they reach a saturation point. I closely followed an IT SPO that created waves in the IT services market decades ago in terms of its growth. This IT SPO started with less than $1.8 million USD in year-on-year revenue, and within 20 years, it has reached nearly $8 billion in year-on-year revenue; this illustrates its meteoric growth over this period. But today, this organization is achieving revenue growth that is merely on par with its peer IT SPOs.

The Bottom Line

The *bottom line* is an IT SPO's income after all expenses have been deducted from revenues. It is also referred as the *profit margin*.

The bottom line describes how efficient an IT SPO is with respect to its spending and operating costs and how effectively it controls total costs. Typically, IT SPOs measure two aspects with respect to the financial results: the contribution margin and the profit margin.

Definitions   The *contribution margin* is the difference between revenue and direct costs.

The *profit margin* is the difference between revenue and direct costs plus indirect costs.

Several research projects have indicated that pure players typically manage to achieve year-on-year profit margins between 20% and 25%, whereas multinational IT SPOs operate between 10% and 17%. The HFS Global IT Service Provider Organization Ranking 2013 listed the profit margins that each IT SPO achieved in 2013, as shown in Table 2-2.

Table 2-2. Estimated Profit Margins by IT SPO in 2013[2, 3]

Service Provider	Est. Profit Margin
IBM	17.9%
Fujitsu	5.9%
HP	2.8%
Accenture	15.3%
NTT	4.7%
SAP	N/A
Oracle	N/A
Capgemini	8.3%
CSC	8.9%
TCS	28.4%
Top 10	**11.5%**
Cognizant	19.0%
Infosys	23.5%
Wipro	21.3%
HCL	22.2%
Total Market	**100%**

Direct Costs

Direct costs can be either fixed or variable; hence, it is essential for a project manager to understand both fixed and variable costs in order to arrive at the correct baseline of contribution margins. Staff time booked to a project is a fixed cost; variable costs include travel and staff expenses that are directly related to the project.

---

[2]HfS Research, estimated from supplier financials, 2014, HfS Research Limited.
[3]Revenues are fitted to the nearest calendar year. Profit margins are calculated from the nearest margin in published financials. SAP and Oracle margins are not included, because these IT SPOs do not publish pure services profit margins.

▧ **Definition**   A *resource bench* or *bench* in the IT services industry indicates a pool of people in an IT SPO who are available for the next assignment and currently are not being utilized for any tasks. They may have been removed from their respective projects because the projects ended or there is no further opportunity to use them in those projects. Every IT SPO maintains a resource bench to ensure that new projects can be staffed in a timely manner. This is similar to a manufacturing organization that keeps investing to be sure it always has some excess factory capacity that can be used if an order suddenly flows in.

Indirect Costs

Indirect costs are other non-billable costs such as business development, overhead, recruitment, learning and development, administration, and security. These expenses affect the organization as a whole, not just a project or a product.

Indirect costs are also referred to as the "real costs" of doing business. They include items such as advertising and marketing, general firm supplies, accounting services, payroll, the cost of maintaining resource bench, and the cost of real estate, such as office rent. These constitute the overhead of maintaining the entire organization; hence, indirect costs are calculated as a percentage of a project, which is then used to calculate the profit margin of the project.

Like direct costs, indirect costs can be both fixed or variable. Fixed costs include items such as rent paid for the organization's building. Variable costs include such things as electricity and gas, and the cost of the resource bench.

IT SPO Accountability for the Top and Bottom Lines

Accountability is defined as the obligation of an individual or organization to account for its activities, accept responsibility for them, and disclose the results in a transparent manner. It also includes the responsibility for money or other entrusted property.

A successful IT SPO mandates accountability for one task to one person rather than to a group of individuals. Establishing a clear matrix of roles and responsibilities in cross-functional/departmental projects and processes is essential for an organization to be successful. Several roles have been defined that are responsible for managing different areas of an organization's business in an IT SPO; these include group CEO, sales force, delivery team / delivery management, practice head, regional head, practice solution team, practice delivery team, support group CEO, and function lead.

Group CEO

The responsibilities of an IT SPO's CEO are set by the organization's board of directors or other authority, depending on the organization's legal structure. Typically, the CEO has responsibilities as director, decision maker, leader, manager, and executor. The decision-making role involves high-level decisions about policy and strategy for the organization.

As a leader of the organization, the CEO advises the board of directors, motivates employees, and drives change in the organization. As a manager, the CEO presides over the organization's day-to-day operations.

Sales Force

As discussed in Chapter 1, the sales force is a team of individuals who are accountable for generating revenue (which is called as the top-line target) by selling their organization's services to new and existing customers. A sales team also works together to increase brand awareness and drive sales forward.

In addition to generating income, individuals from the sales force are responsible for building trust with customers. Sales representatives engage customers at all stages of the relationship. New customers require interaction with organization representatives and opportunities to learn about the brand. Current customers gain trust through consistent follow-up and communication with sales representatives. Sales representatives also work to reengage previous customers through promotions, discounts, and communications. Building trust throughout the customer sales cycle increases customer satisfaction. Hence, in some IT SPOs, sales personnel are also referred to as *client partners, relationship managers*, or *client executives*.

In most IT SPOs, sales-force teams have very little accountability related to the bottom–line growth.

Delivery Team / Delivery Management

Individuals from delivery teams are accountable for ensuring that projects are delivered within the defined period, at a specified quality and cost. They manage day-to-day project execution. From the organization's financial perspective, delivery-management personnel are accountable for the project's contribution margins.

The delivery team includes different roles such as project managers, delivery managers, and delivery heads. Each role has its own set of responsibilities.

Vertical and Sub-vertical Head

Vertical and sub-vertical heads, also referred to as profit-and loss heads (P&L heads), have accountability for both top-line and bottom-line growth, meaning the revenue and profit margin within the purview of their business. Both the sales team and the delivery team directly report to the vertical and/or the sub-vertical head, based on their scope of business in the IT SPO. This role is accountable for ensuring that indirect costs are maintained at a reasonable level and that appropriate money is spent on business development and training, as well as development of human resources, within the vertical.

An individual in this role is supposed to drive sales processes effectively and ensure that the unit is profitable by delivering results to customers within specified parameters related to cost, quality, and schedule.

Practice Head

As discussed in Chapter 1, a *practice* is a subject matter unit in an IT SPO. The core responsibility of this unit is to ensure that individuals from the practice sell their respective services to existing and new customers across verticals.

A practice head is accountable for revenue, which is a direct indication of how the specific practice is generating business value for the organization. The practice head is accountable for ensuring that indirect costs are maintained at a reasonable level and that appropriate money is spent on business development, as well as training and development of human resources, within the vertical.

In addition, the practice head is accountable for innovation, which entails making sure market trends are analyzed in the subject matter area to enhance existing offerings and create new offerings to be competitive in the market.

Regional Head

Tier-1 and Tier-2 IT SPOs typically reach customers across geographies instead of limiting themselves to specific geographies. This is because they want to tap opportunities across the globe and increase their business. For such an IT SPO in a practice structure, a practice lead is made accountable for one or multiple related geographies; their core responsibility is revenue generation and business development with existing and new clients by collaborating with the vertical teams.

Typically, this role is held by a person who is technically knowledgeable in the subject matter area along and has a detailed understanding of the overall services the practice offers, because the regional head is required to sell services pertaining to the practice subject matter area.

Practice Solution Team

A practice solution team is a team of experts who are responsible for driving the creation of new offerings and enhancing existing offerings. They are also part of the team that provides technical support for any business proposal made to customers in their respective subject matter area. Typically, this team is considered hands-on in their subject matter area.

Practice Delivery Team

As the name implies, delivery teams deliver the actual output to the customer once a deal is finalized. Practice delivery teams are groups who are technically hands-on in their subject matter area and work on associated projects. Individuals from delivery teams are accountable for ensuring that projects are delivered within the defined time period, and at a specified quality and cost.

A practice delivery team includes different roles such as developers, designers, testers, business architects, and technical architects who are proficient in their respective subject matter areas. This team is typically a superset of the practice solutions team.

Support Group CEO

The support group CEO has several responsibilities, depending on the size of the IT SPO and the different entities that form the support group entity. However, at a basic level, a support group CEO is accountable for ensuring that verticals and horizontals are receiving support from all departments in a timely manner, based on which they are able to achieve their targets. For example, the support group CEO needs to ensure that the legal group is providing advice to verticals and horizontals during the deal-creation process and during project execution about aspects related to legal compliance, based on the organization's standards.

In addition to these core responsibilities, a support group CEO is also accountable for ensuring that indirect costs are maintained at a reasonable level and that adequate support is provided to all required personnel in the IT SPO, such as the verticals and horizontals.

Function Lead

A function lead is accountable for one of various functions within the support group. The function lead is responsible for ensuring that verticals and horizontals are receiving support from the lead's department in the required subject matter area in a timely manner.

For example, one of the roles of the support function involves human resources. The function lead of the human resource department must ensure that the lead's group identifies the human resource needs of the IT SPO in collaboration with each vertical and horizontal of the organization. Recruitment is performed to fulfill the resource needs of verticals and horizontals. In addition to recruitment, the function lead of the human resource department is responsible for managing employee welfare and motivation, labor-management relations, and implementing human resource policies.

Because most of the staff members in this group do not generate direct revenue, the organization's indirect costs are affected. Therefore, in addition to their core responsibilities, a function lead is also accountable for ensuring that indirect costs are well managed within specified limits.

Differentiators among IT SPOs

Every IT SPO, regardless of size, wishes to create at least one differentiating theme that can act as a catalyst for its growth and identify it uniquely in the market space. In my nearly two-decade career in IT, I have closely followed and worked with several Tier-1, Tier-2, and Tier-3 pure players and multinational IT SPOs. Recollecting these experiences, I have summarized my insights here:

- One Tier-1 IT SPO is well known and prides itself on having the best client-facing managers. The result is that customers are able to rely heavily on staff that this organization deploys in client-facing roles.

- Another IT SPO I know prides itself on having the best business expertise, whether in the banking domain, manufacturing, or the retail industry, because its strategy is to recruit and attract business talent from only top business schools across the world. This means most customers receive the best advice from this organization's staff regarding core business-related transactions.

- I know another IT SPO that has won several large deals based on its employees' strength in speaking the local language in the local market. This organization has blended well into the India offshoring business and has established itself in the industry as the best IT SPO to blend the local culture with offshore partners. This means customers can use the best local talent in client-facing roles and can take full advantage of talent from developing countries, which provides a cost advantage.

- Another IT SPO I know is considered the "cost saving" organization due to its expertise in working with a large pool of talent in developing countries, thereby providing cost advantages and efficient availability of resources to customers.

- Several Tier-3 IT SPOs have created unique differentiators for themselves. One is known globally for its expertise in executing projects using agile methodology; every project in this IT SPO is managed using this approach. Another IT SPO is well known for its unique services using cloud computing technology; it only conducts business related to cloud services. It prides itself on having the best talent in the cloud subject matter area, and its employees have in-depth technical knowledge.

All the IT SPOs I have discussed have created a unique trademark in the IT services industry. But unfortunately, most have not been able to achieve the distinction of being *innovative* organizations. An innovative IT SPO is an organization in which each member constantly strives to identify opportunities from which their client can benefit.

Key Points

- The top line refers to an IT SPO's gross sales or revenue.

- Growing Tier-2 or Tier-3 IT SPOs post growth from 20% to as much as 300% year-on-year until they reach a saturation point.

- The bottom line is an IT SPO's income after all expenses have been deducted from revenues.

- Typically, the CEO has responsibilities as a director, a decision maker, a leader, a manager, and an executor. The decision-making role involves high-level decisions about policy and strategy for the IT SPO.

- The sales force is a team of individuals who are accountable for generating income and revenue by selling their IT SPO's services to new and existing customers.

- Individuals from delivery teams are accountable for ensuring that projects are delivered within the defined period, at a specified quality and cost.

- Vertical and sub-vertical heads, also referred to as profit-and-loss heads (P&L heads), are accountable for both top-line and bottom-line growth, meaning the revenue and profit margin within the purview of their business.

- A practice is a subject matter unit in an IT SPO. The core responsibility of this unit is to ensure that individuals from the practice sell their respective services to existing and new customers across verticals.

- A support group CEO is accountable for ensuring that verticals and horizontals are receiving support from all departments in a timely manner, based on which they are able to achieve their targets.

- A function lead is accountable for one of various functions within the support group.

IT Service Provider Organizations' Tactics and Tricks for Hitting P&L Targets

All IT services provider organizations (SPOs) have the same strategic goals: to increase the top line and to manage the bottom line effectively. To achieve these goals and related targets, each IT SPO defines its own strategies. Most of these revolve around human resources, because the IT industry is driven by its employees and their capabilities.

Every IT SPO aspires to do the following:

- Build a capable and proud team that enthusiastically provides excellent services for customers

- Recruit, retain, and compensate staff competitively to achieve the business goals of the organization

- Provide excellent customer service that leaves every customer with a lasting positive impression of the organization

- Provide compelling services that are convenient for customers to find and use

- Use current and innovative information/communications technology to provide access to services, resources, and programs

- reach and influence customers to purchase services from them

All of these factors directly or indirectly have an effect on achieving the IT SPO's strategic goals—which are, as stated previously, to increase the top line and to manage the bottom line effectively. However, each IT SPO has its own quantitative targets for these two parameters. Some IT SPOs have a very aggressive strategy for increasing their top line; in contrast, other organizations assertively try to improve their bottom line. Some have aggressive targets for both. This chapter provides examples of such targets that I have gathered from the past several years of research.

Top Line

Typically, at an organizational level, Tier-1 IT SPOs forecast themselves as having a steady increase in revenue growth of between 20% and 25% year on year. Some multinational IT SPOs maintain their estimates of year on year revenue growth at between 12% and 14%. These targets are at the organization level; within the organization, the targets differ from vertical to vertical and from horizontal to horizontal based on the business potential and market share of the IT SPO. Targets for each IT SPO entity, such as a vertical or a horizontal, and even for accounts within a vertical or horizontal, are defined based on market potential, organizational strength, and current market share.

Consider, for example, a pure player IT SPO named Organization A. In 2013, 30% of its revenue ($1.328 million) originated from the US banking sub-vertical, which belongs to the banking and financial services vertical. Figure 3-1 provides a breakdown of 2013 revenue achievements, based on which 2014 targets are defined for the banking vertical.

Vertical	Banking and Financial Services
Business Unit	Banking
Regional Business Unit	Banking - US
2013 Revenue	$1,328.50
2014 Revenue Target (%)	15.10%
2014 Revenue Target ($ value)	$1,529.10

Geography	Client Name	Revenue 2013 (in million $)	Total IT Spent (Customer wise)	Company A Market Share	Competitors Market Share (%) / Market Potential	Revenue Target 2014 (in %)	Revenue Target 2014 (in million $)
Banking BU - US Geography	Client A	$410.0	$1,500	27.3%	72.7%	21.0%	$496.10
	Client B	$340.0	$1,000	34.0%	66.0%	10.0%	$374.00
	Client C	$300.0	$800	37.5%	62.5%	15.0%	$345.00
	Client D	$140.0	$400	35.0%	65.0%	0.0%	$140.00
	Client E	$120.0	$350	34.3%	65.7%	5.0%	$126.00
	Client F	$8.0	$400	2.0%	98.0%	20.0%	$9.60
	Client G	$4.0	$200	2.0%	98.0%	20.0%	$4.80
	Client H	$3.4	$80	4.3%	95.8%	50.0%	$5.10
	Client I	$3.1	$20	15.5%	84.5%	45.0%	$4.50
	Client J	$0.0	$100	0.0%	100.0%	10.0%	$0.00
	Client K	$0.0	$2,000	0.0%	100.0%	20.0%	$0.00
	Client L	$0.0	$180	0.0%	100.0%	5.0%	$0.00
	Client M	$0.0	$380	0.0%	100.0%	10.0%	$0.00
	Client N	$0.0	$200	0.0%	100.0%	15.0%	$0.00
	Other Unknown Clients		$1,200	0.0%	100.0%	2.0%	$24.00
Total		$1,329	$8,810	15%	85%	15.10%	$1,529.10

Figure 3-1. Breakdown of 2013 revenues and revenue targets for Organization A's banking US vertical

Different elements are considered when defining the targets for each account and for the business unit. This is an exercise performed at the end of every year by analyzing the details of areas such as the market potential of the specific line of business in IT, the current IT SPO market share, competitors' market share, the IT potential of each customer, competitor analysis, relationships with existing customers, and other factors.

As an example for Organization A, revenue targets were defined based on two categories of customers:

- *Existing customers:* A percentage of the growth target is assigned to each client, such as a revenue target of a 21% increase above 2013 revenue for Client A, and a revenue target of a 10% increase above 2013 revenue for Client B. The percentage of the target increase is determined based on various influencing factors (for example, the type of work currently being performed and the relationship with the customer). This target is typically assigned to the sales team.

- *New customers:* A percentage of the growth target is assigned to the sales team. Their job is to mine the existing market and identify new customers.

Almost all IT SPOs have a large portion of revenues coming from so-called *revenue-generating engines* or *flagship fields*. Some examples include the following:

- Verticals such as banking and financial services, insurance, health care, and retail

- Horizontals such as core technologies (Java, .NET, mainframe, in-demand technologies, and so on); infrastructure services; social, media, analytics, and cloud (SMAC); and consulting

- Customers who contribute more than 5% of overall organization revenue

Individuals accountable for these revenue-generating engines have revenue targets that are greater than the organizational targets in many cases, although exceptions exist. I have been accountable for such revenue-generating engines in four instances during my career, with targets between 20% and 50% revenue growth year on year (based on the potential of business growth in these areas). Profit margin targets varied between 18% and 25% from assignment to assignment.

These revenue-generating engines have high visibility at the CEO level; performance of each area of the business is reviewed by the CEO on a monthly basis. Customer relationships at the executive level also are managed by the CEO in many instances.

At the organization level, revenue-generating engines are identified and an appropriate focus is maintained to ensure that long-term revenue and profitability are achieved. This approach is cascaded and adapted at lower levels of the IT SPO: the CEOs of the verticals and horizontals also create revenue-generating engines based on their area of focus, similar to those defined at the organization level, with targets for growth and profitability year on year. This makes the IT SPO strategy and approach consistent across the organization. For example, in Figure 3-1, the banking vertical of the US region could define Client A, Client B, and Client C as its revenue-generating engines.

Revenue-generating engines are the basis on which any IT SPO can maintain steady success; every IT SPO aspires to continually create revenue-generating engines. Organizations focus on customers, verticals, and horizontals, all which have business and market potential; and appropriate strategies are created at each level within the IT SPO to convert such potential to actuality.

Bottom Line

The bottom-line target is an interesting topic to address. Each IT SPO has its own targets and its own method of managing profit margins.

The HFS Global IT Service Provider Ranking 2013 listed the profit margins achieved by IT service providers in 2013. These values are presented in Table 2-2 of Chapter 2. Although every IT SPO seeks to achieve high profit margins, the organizations' targets and achievements differ. Multinational IT SPOs typically achieve low profit margins, as compared with pure players. There are several reasons why multinational IT SPOs tend to deliver lower profit margins, some of which are listed here:

- A large percentage of the workforce, including senior management, is located in developed countries, thereby affecting the profit margins negatively.

- Resource benches are maintained at onsite locations, which are typically in developed countries.

- Investments in research and development and marketing are more significant.

- They have higher selling and general administrative (S&GA) costs.

- A large portion of work is performed onsite at development centers in developed countries.

Although the profit-margin achievements of different IT SPOs are unique, a key aspect for discussion involves the targets that these organizations aim to achieve year on year. Certain IT SPOs attempt to achieve impossible targets, which affects their reputation in the market and reduces the quality they deliver to their clients. The worst actions are often are taken by IT SPOs during periods of recession. As an example, during the 2008-2009 recession, I encountered several IT SPOs that cut jobs to maintain their profit margins, to the extent that the cuts affected the long-term success of the entire organization. After significant job cuts at all levels, including senior management, the organizations were unable to attract and retain the best talent after the recession ended. Even today, this situation continues, with an average attrition rate of more than 20% in these organizations. They took these actions to maintain their profit-margin targets but ended up doing long-term harm to themselves.

Some IT SPOs make employees compromise their quality of life by accepting projects with impossible timelines and low costs. To achieve the specified margins, teams are required to work long spans of weekends; such organizations are well known to many of us. Although they meet their financial targets year on year, the fate of such IT SPOs is not secure in the long term. In contrast, other IT SPOs are considered preferred employers.

It is important to note that low profit margins do not necessarily indicate a healthy organization. Having a low profit margin does not imply that an IT SPOs provides a high quality of life to its employees or that customers are satisfied. A sustainable IT SPO is one that manages its bottom line to the extent that it is profitable and offers development opportunities to its employees, thereby retaining them and providing the utmost quality of services to its customers.

Contribution Margins : an Enabler for Profitability

One element that contributes to the achievement of profit margins is the contribution margin, which is directly related to the profitability of a specific project. A pure player IT SPO typically achieves a contribution margin higher than that of a multinational IT SPO; at a broad level, these organizations tend to achieve contribution margins between 40% and 60%.

The contribution margins of pure player IT SPOs and multinational IT SPOs vary for several reasons. Following are two of the top factors:

- The operating model of multinational IT SPOs tends to maintain a large percentage of employees onsite (in developed countries or geographies) due to their geographical base. In contrast, pure player IT SPOs have only client-facing and sales staff in developed countries, which has a direct effect on the organizations' indirect costs.

- Pure player IT SPOs today tend to make a precise correlation between the level of an employee in the organization and the role they perform. An employee is never allowed to perform a job that is below their level in the organization. This is in contrast to multinational IT SPOs. I have seen several cases in multinational IT SPOs where, for example, an experienced 25-year vice president was managing a 500,000 Euro project. This has a direct effect on the contribution margins of the project.

Almost all pure player IT SPOs maintain a resource bench averaging between 15% and 20%. Most of the resources on the bench are stationed in developing geographies. In contrast, multinational IT SPOs tend to maintain a relatively low bench, in the range of 5% to 10%, and resources are spread across developed and developing countries. This is one of the reasons pure player IT SPOs can easily staff a large number of resources within a short timeframe, primarily to work from developing countries.

The current reality with respect to multinational IT SPOs is that they have high indirect costs, primarily due to maintaining a high onsite presence. But these IT SPOs are now taking steps to reduce their costs, on par with their peer organizations. Most of these organizations have opened new offices in developing countries to use a global talent pool and reduce costs via offshoring.

Tricks for Improving the Bottom Line

Different IT SPOs and leaders adopt a variety of techniques in order to be profitable. Although some of these techniques are efficient as components of healthy organizational policy, others negatively affect the organization in the long run, even if they permit the organization to achieve short-term benefits. Following are a few of these techniques adopted by organizations or their staff:

- *Reducing the bench:* The end-of-year pressure to achieve profit-margin targets is enormous, especially for senior executives in an IT SPO. One area of focus that I see constantly involves reducing the resource bench to achieve a higher gross operating profit (GOP) for the financial year. IT SPOs that are under pressure to meet financial targets apply different techniques to achieve their goals, ranging from deploying high-profile employees to low-end jobs to taking the very drastic step of firing employees. Yes—as mentioned earlier, several IT SPOs I know of have done this, and they have reduced their business share in the market because of these misguided short-term actions.

- *Pyramid management:* I am aware of several IT SPOs that use a very lean pyramid structure—they have a high percentage of inexperienced employees and resources with medium levels of experience on the team. I have seen projects with a mandate at the organizational level to deploy 45% of *freshers* (defined in a moment) in every project. This has an effect on direct costs, and, initially, such projects can show healthy contribution margins. However, trying to optimize the pyramid to an extent that impacts the quality of project delivery always leads to failure.

- *Locale management:* In the current business environment, the percentages of resources distributed between low-cost and high-cost geographies are highly dependent on customers and their respective geographies, as well as the type of work being performed. However, this also depends on the particular IT SPO.

▓ **Definitions**   A *pyramid* in an IT services organization is the ratio of experienced (highly experienced, medium experience) vs. inexperienced resources (resources with no experience) deployed on client projects. Typically, this ratio is calculated based on the level of an individual or designation of an individual within the IT SPO, because the cost of an individual is derived from their level or designation as an employee. The bottom 90% to 95% of the pyramid are generally the individuals who actually deliver the project, such as the designers, developers, and testers. The top 5% to 10% of the pyramid consists of project management staff.

Resources with zero experience, also referred to as *freshers*, are employees who joined an IT SPO from college and have undergone basic training in specific technologies. These employees are deployed on projects that also use experienced staff, which aids the freshers in gaining experience. As an example, some IT SPOs deploy 25% highly experienced employees, 55% medium experienced employees, and 20% freshers for a project.

Locale is the ratio of employees working in low-cost geographies (developing countries) to those working in high-cost geographies (developed countries) for a project. Locale management involves managing this ratio.

Most pure player IT SPOs have more than 60% of staff working from low-cost geographies, and some organizations aim to increase this number to improve their margins.

Key Points

- Tier-1 organizations forecast themselves as having a steady increase in revenue (top line) growth of between 20% and 25% year on year.

- At an organizational level, some multinational organizations maintain their estimates of year-on-year revenue (top line) increases at between 12% and 14%.

- A pure player IT SPO typically achieves a contribution margin higher than that of a multinational IT SPO. At a broad level, organizations tend to achieve contribution margins between 40% and 60%.

- Almost all pure player IT SPOs maintain a resource bench averaging between 15% and 20%. Most of the resources on the bench are stationed in developing geographies.

- Multinational IT SPOs tend to maintain a relatively low bench as compared to pure player IT SPOs, in the range of 5% to 10%. Resources are spread across developed and developing countries.

- A pyramid in an IT SPO is the ratio of experienced (highly experienced, medium experience) vs. inexperienced resources (resources with no experience) deployed on client projects.

- Zero-experience resources (also referred to as *freshers*) are employees who joined an IT SPO from college and have undergone basic training on specific technologies.

- Locale is the ratio of employees working in low-cost geographies (developing countries) to those working in high-cost geographies (developed countries) for a project. Locale management involves managing this ratio.

The Operational Parameters of IT Service Providers

For a business to survive, growth is an imperative, not an option. Nearly all IT SPOs have a common thread that binds them together and makes them different from companies producing material goods: they sell services. These services have the following characteristics:

- They are always designed to fit a broader customer base and are tailored for customers based on their individual needs.

- Most services rely on human resources, which means that, in the majority of cases, customers buy skills and competency resources from the IT SPO.

The idea that companies must always value their customers has become so common that managers, especially in IT SPOs, rarely question it. Nevertheless, those who have examined how revenue-generating engines and customers of revenue-generating engines are treated by their IT SPOs can understand that the strategy adopted by IT SPO executives to value these customers is unique; it entails over-the-top service. This is one of the reasons these companies are able to retain their position with these customer bases and grow their businesses along with the customers. A successful IT SPO replicates this behavior across all of its customers, regardless of the size of the customers' transactions.

Customers tend to punish bad service more than they reward praiseworthy service. This mean loyalty has a lot more to do with how well companies deliver on their basic promises than with how dazzling the service experience might be. Moreover, bad service has ripple effects that can perpetuate the company's reputation for years. I had a personal experience with one of the largest banks in Europe; we failed to demonstrate our commitment to this customer in 2005, and until recently we were not able to grow our business with this customer by even 1%.

Two core pillars for the success of any IT SPO are having competent, motivated, loyal resources both to sell and to deliver results; and having unique, strong offerings in the organization's specialized area of business. Numerous organizations have been successful and have reached the billion-dollar revenue mark based on these two pillars.

The strategy of every IT SPO is achieved by implementing these two aspects. This chapter discusses how IT SPOs approach them.

Performance Management of Human Capital

Performance management is the process of creating a work environment that can yield the best performance from employees. It is a comprehensive work system that begins when a job is defined according to specified requirements. It ends when an employee leaves an organization.

Many individuals consider performance management to be the process of appraising an individual, but it is broader than that. A successful organization is able to retain talent even during the harshest business conditions, and very few organizations achieve this. Organizations that can maintain high employee focus are known as the "best employers to work for" and also achieve superior revenue figures in the market space.

Most IT SPO classifies its employees into four categories: top performers (the top 10%), good performers (the next 30%), average performers (the next 40%), and low performers (the final 20%). The appraisal system often uses the same procedure of classifying employee performance based on these four categories. However, in current IT SPOs, performance management is not bulletproof. In some cases, even very high performers are left behind due to organizational and managerial politics. For example, misuse of the appraisal process occurs in during difficult economic conditions when organizations use performance management as a yardstick to terminate employees who are resources on the bench, for the purpose of making profits in the short term.

Jack Welch's vitality model is described as a *20-70-10 system*. In this model, the top 20% of employees are referred to as highly productive, whereas the bottom 10% are categorized as nonperformers who need to be fired from the organization.[1, 2] This is the principle followed by most IT SPOs.

Competitive Positioning and Accommodation of Client Requirements

Very few IT SPOs venture into areas in which they are not experts. There are also very few IT sales executives who tell their customers that they do not have expertise in a specific function. Instead, these executives provide their customers with a roadmap, describing how they can build their skills to perform the functions in which they currently are not experienced.

I have often heard from sales executives, "Let's first sell, and then we will see how to deliver." The reason for such a statement is that in most IT SPOs, sales teams are not accountable for delivering what they promise. Another reason is the hard targets sales executives carry to increase revenue. But such sales executives are never ultimately successful: although they may achieve initial victories by winning deals based on false claims, when they cannot deliver, failure is inevitable. News of failure spreads faster than news of success. Superior sales executives pursue business that their organization can deliver, and organizations constantly try to achieve expertise in areas in which they lack experience.

IT SPOs follow two types of selling processes: traditional selling and consultative selling. *Traditional selling* involves a product your organization makes. In other words, personnel from an IT SPO attempt to match customer requirements with the products and services the company presently specializes in. In simple terms, the organization sells its products and services to the customer.

Consultative sales entail understanding the customer business, assessing the customer's competitive market, listing the customer's challenges, and mapping the customer's business against its competitors. Once sufficient knowledge of these topics has been acquired, existing organizational services can be tailored to the customer's needs, and the selling process begins.

---

[1]Alan Murray, "Should I Rank My Employees?" *Wall Street Journal*, http://guides.wsj.com/management/recruiting-hiring-and-firing/should-i-rank-my-employees/.
[2]Del Jones, "Let People Know Where They Stand, Welch Says: Ranking Workers Pays, Former GE Chief Says," *USA Today*, April 18, 2005, http://usatoday30.usatoday.com/educate/college/careers/Advice/advice4-18-05.htm.

Today, most leading IT SPOs want to engage in consultative selling, but few of them have had notable success. Nevertheless, organizations that constantly strive to sell via the consultative mode are most preferred by their customers.

In the article "The Big O—Outcome Selling," author Tom Pisello says that buyers expect value-added selling rather than traditional selling, which implies that being sold standard products or services is not an area of interest for buyers. Buyers are more interested in knowing how their business can benefit from each of the IT SPO's services.[3] At the Forrester Technology Sales Enablement Forum,[4] Forrester introduced an umbrella term to describe these practices: *outcome selling*. Using this approach, IT SPOs design their value communications system to optimize the value their customers realize. This concept is closely related to consultative selling.

Working Modalities between IT Service Providers and Receivers

Working with customers is cultural. Sales employees from some geographies always say "Yes," regardless of whether they can deliver or not. Employees from other cultures always say "Maybe," even when they are certain they can deliver. Preferred IT SPOs train their employees to say "Yes" only when they are sure to deliver and to say "No" when they are certain that they cannot deliver under any circumstances.

Employees of IT SPOs are always under pressure to satisfy their customers. Some of them lose the trust of their customers because they are not able to deliver what the customer asked for.

Attrition

In today's competitive business environment, the effects of attrition on employees can be detrimental to both the bottom line and to the quality of service provided to the customer. Attrition can involve the loss of employees or the loss of customers. It is a common phenomenon in any organization. IT SPOs typically experience large effects due to attrition because this industry is based on the strengths and capabilities of employees.

---

[3]Tom Pisello, "The Big O—Outcome Selling," March 15, 2011, Alinean, http://blog.alinean.com/2011/03/big-o-outcome-selling.html.
[4]Bradford Holmes, "Lessons from Forrester's Inaugural Technology Sales Enablement Forum," Forrester, http://blogs.forrester.com/bradford_holmes/11-02-18-lessons_from_forresters_innagural_technology_sales_enablement_forum.

Today, average attrition levels across organizations are between 10% and 12%, and many IT SPOs understand that attrition is one of the measures by which a company's quality of service is determined. Some organizations struggle to maintain industry-average attrition levels; this is because in the past, executives made the mistake of adopting policies that conflicted with employee morale. Once a wave of discomfort is created across a broad group of employees, it has a ripple effect for several years. You must follow a completely different and drastic approach at an organizational level to return attrition levels to normal.

Productivity

In today's IT economy, software development is a significant expense for most organizations, so lagging software-development productivity can have a significant effect on an organization's ability to compete and survive. Many organizations believe that their software development is not optimized; others believe that theirs is highly optimized. Some people at senior levels still consider software development to be a cost center with poorly understood processes and deliverables. However, without improved efficiency, it is difficult to achieve results which are cost-effective.

Definition *Productivity* is a measure based on which the efficiency of producing software is measured. It is defined as the ratio of output units of software produced to the input units of effort.[5, 6, 7]

To ensure that software development is efficient, productivity needs to be measured. IT SPOs continually adapt new techniques to improve the productivity of their teams. There are different methods for measuring productivity; one of the most popular is the *functional sizing method*, also called *function point analysis* (FPA). Another means of measuring productivity is by the number of lines of code written.

---

[5]Walt Scacchi, "Understanding Software Productivity," in *Software Engineering and Knowledge Engineering: Trends for the Next Decade*, ed. William D. Hurley (World Scientific Press, 1995).
[6]Stefan Wagner and Melanie Ruhe, "A Systematic Review of Productivity Factors in Software Development," Technische Universität München, 2008.
[7]E. Nwelih and I. F. Amadin, "Modeling Software Reuse in Traditional Productivity Model," *Asian Journal of Information Technology* 7, no. 11 (2008), 484-488.

Definition *Function points* measure software from a functional perspective. In this method, project requirements are broken down into smaller units called *functions*. Based on an empirical process model, the effort required to develop each function is estimated.

Using this method, productivity is measured as the ratio between the function points and the actual hours spent working on a project.

To derive function points, benchmarking figures from the International Software Benchmarking Standards Group (ISBSG) are used.[8] The ISBSG report is based on data collected by the organization. The ISBSG repository now contains data from more than 5,400 completed projects from around the world. Table 4-1 lists some ISBSG benchmarks.

Table 4-1. Function Point Benchmarks (Number of Hours/FP)

Language	N	Min	P10	P25	Median (P50) # of hours/FP	P75	P90	Max	Mean	Std Dev
C#	42	1.9	6.1	9.6	15.1	25.1	39.7	49.8	18.8	12.8
Java	171	1.9	4.8	5.9	8.0	15.6	29.4	74.2	13.3	12.9
Power builder	19	4.2	5.0	6.4	9.3	14.1	18.6	23.6	10.9	5.6
SQL	60	2.4	3.9	6.2	11.4	16.7	27.2	55.5	13.5	10.7

In the table,

- N is the number of projects or data instances in the sample.
- Min is the minimum value found in the sample.
- Pxx is the xxth percentile and is the value that is greater than the values of 10% of the members of the sample or subsample.
- Median (sometimes written P50) is the middle value; half the values in the data sample or subsample are less than this value, and the other half are greater than this value.
- Max is the maximum value found in the sample.

---

[8]ISBSG, *Practical Software Project Estimation*, 3rd ed., ed. Peter R. Hill (McGraw-Hill Osborne Media, 2011).

- Mean is the arithmetic mean or average of the value found in the sample.

- Std Dev is the standard deviation.

As an example, for a project to be developed using C# language, Table 4-1 indicates that SPOs must deliver each function point within 15.1 hours, which is the productivity measure for C# language.

The productivity figures in the ISBSG report for each language are calculated as a summation on activity phases such as planning, specifications, design, building, testing, and implementation:

- *Planning phase:* Set the time and cost for a project by going into the details of the project requirements.

- *Specification phase:* Detail project requirements, both technically and functionally.

- *Design phase:* Translate technical and functional requirements into conceptual models.

- *Building phase:* Develop software based on the designs and technical and functional specifications.

- *Testing phase:* Test the developed software.

- *Implementation phase:* Deploy the tested software to production.

The ratios between these activity phases are presented in Table 4-2.

Table 4-2. Breakdown of Productivity Figures in the ISBSG Report[9] divided by Phases

Phase	Enhancements
Plan	8%
Specification	16%
Build	50%
Test	20%
Implement	6%

---

[9]ISBSG publication *Practical Software Project Estimation* 3rd Edition [2011]

As an example, for a project to be developed using java language, Table 4-1 indicates that SPOs must deliver each function point within 8 hours, which is the productivity measure for java language. As depicted in Table 4-3, this productivity measure, once decomposed at a activity phase level, indicates that for each function point, panning should be completed in 0.64 hours, specifications should be completed in 1.28 hours, build should be completed in 4 hours, test in 1.6 hours and implementation in 0.48 hours.

Table 4-3. Breakdown of Productivity Figures for java language divided by Phases

Phase	Percentage	Hours
Plan	8%	0.64
Specification	16%	1.28
Build	50%	4
Test	20%	1.6
Implement	6%	0.48

Although function points form one of the measures to estimate the size of software projects, with benchmarks to measure productivity, not all projects can be sized using function points, which mean not all projects can measure productivity using this model. IT SPOs adapt different techniques to measure productivity, and it is very important for service receiver organizations to understand these approaches; productivity baselines can be established based on them.

Key Points

- Performance management is the process of creating a work environment that can yield the best performance from employees.

- Most IT SPOs classify their employees into four categories: top performers (the highest 10%), good performers (the next 30%), average performers (the next 40%), and low performers (the final 20%).

- Traditional selling involves a product your organization makes. In other words, personnel from an IT SPO attempt to match customer requirements with the products and services the company presently specializes in.

- Consultative sales entail understanding the customer's business, assessing the customer's competitive market, listing the customer's challenges, and mapping the customer's business with their competitors. Once sufficient knowledge of these topics has been acquired, existing organizational services can be tailored to the customer's needs, and the selling process begins.

- Average attrition levels across organizations are between 10% and 12%, and many IT SPOs understand that attrition is one of the measures based on which their quality of service is determined.

- Productivity is an average measure of the efficiency of production. Traditionally, productivity in software development is defined as a ratio of output units produced to the input units of effort.

- IT SPOs adapt different techniques to measure productivity. It is very important for service receiver organizations to understand these approaches; productivity baselines can be established based on them.

Unleashing the Full Potential of Your IT Service Providers

Part I discussed how IT SPOs are structured, their goals and targets, and the way they operate their business. It also discussed how governance is structured within an SPO. With this information, an SRO can enhance its existing SPO organization model.

Part II shows you how to manage your SPOs. Managing these relationships to extract their full potential is the ultimate goal every SRO desires, and the second half of the book provides a variety of guiding principles to achieve this.

It explains the different focus areas in relationships with the SPO, what to expect and what not to expect from an SPO, how to use its strengths and mitigate the risks related to its weaknesses, and how to use this information to get the most out of your SPO.

The essential purpose of this part is to provide SROs with detailed information about how to unleash the full potential of their SPOs. But it is no less essential for SROs to understand that without fully supporting the SPOs, extracting value is not possible. People from SROs and SPOs must work together as teams, jointly and collaboratively meeting challenges impacting either party.

Unleashing the Full Potential of Your IT Service Providers

The Organization of IT Service Receivers

Organizations that want to focus on their core business processes while delegating noncore processes need to select a service provider. In the IT services industry, a business that provides IT services to other organizations is the IT *service provider organization (SPO)*, and the receiver of such services is the IT *service receiver organization (SRO)*. In such a case, personnel from the SRO become customers of the SPO. A person or group from the SPO who sells their organization's services is referred to as a *seller*. Once there is an agreement between a service provider and a service receiver regarding the services to be performed by the SPO, a contract is signed.

IT SROs outsource their IT business to SPOs so they can focus on their core processes while delegating their noncore business (in this case, IT) to an organization with a core business that is IT. As an example, a retail bank is a financial institution with a core business of providing individuals with savings and checking accounts, credit and debit cards, personal loans, mortgage services, and so on. IT is not the bank's core business: the bank does not sell IT services but uses IT as the backbone to perform its core business, which is to serve its investment banking customers.

Another example is Amazon.com, the world's largest online retailer. The company started as an online bookstore and soon began selling video games, electronics, DVDs, CDs, videos and MP3s, food, toys, jewelry, and more. IT is not Amazon's core business, but the company relies heavily on IT to perform its day-to-day business.

Classifying IT Service Receiver Organizations

Similar to IT SPOs, this book defines three broad categories of IT SROs, based on their year-on-year IT spending.

Tier-1 IT SRO

Organizations with an IT budget of more than $1 billion USD year on year are categorized as Tier-1 IT SROs. Typically, these kinds of organizations have their own IT arm; several personnel are deployed to perform IT development. The core focus of this department is to manage and develop some of the company's core IT applications in addition to managing the IT SPOs' outsourced IT work. Such organizations often also maintain IT departments in low-cost countries, to better manage their IT spending. Such IT divisions are referred to as *captives*.

Tier-2 IT SRO

Organizations with an IT budget in the range of $200 million USD to $1 billion USD year on year are categorized as Tier-2 IT SROs. Generally, these organizations have their own IT arm, with several personnel deployed to perform IT development. The core focus of this division is to manage and develop some of the company's core IT applications; the rest are outsourced to IT SPOs. Very few organizations in this category maintain captives.

Tier-3 IT SRO

Organizations with an IT budget of less than $200 million USD year on year are categorized as Tier-3 IT SROs. These organizations have their own IT arm, which is quite small; until a few years ago, such organizations did their IT work in-house. However, given the current market circumstances, where cost is a major driver for all organizations, these companies have started to outsource their IT work. Those that engage an IT SPO maintain a small team of experts to manage the IT SPO in-house and to retain knowledge within the organization. None of these organizations maintain captives.

Captive Centers

Most Tier-1 and Tier-2 SROs establish captives. Company-owned captive operations hold broad appeal because of persistent concerns about intellectual property and security when outsourcing, in addition to the promise they provide for low-cost IT development. Some companies establish captive divisions for contact centers, back office processes such as accounting and research and development, and IT-related work.

Only a few organizations have been successful in managing their captives in the most efficient manner. Several failures have been discussed in the market: for example, I know a couple of Fortune 500 companies that have sold or shut down wholly owned offshore service centers in the last few years.

However, the captive center lives on. Captive activity reached a two-year high in the fourth quarter of 2009, with the opening of 40 new wholly owned service centers offshore, according to outsourcing consultancy Everest, and the last five quarters have seen growth in the captive market.

Captives do succeed in some cases. The keys to their success are defining the right goal for which to establish the captive, investing in achieving that goal, empowering the captive's team to achieve the goal, and making the captive part of the entire organization. I know of several organizations that have succeeded in managing their captives in an integral manner, thereby achieving the desired benefits. Chapter 9 discusses captives in detail.

The Rationale for Outsourcing

Small and midsized companies looking to grow in their core business always desire to keep their focus off noncore businesses, and hence the concept of outsourcing has emerged in the industry. Companies that outsource can focus on their strengths and delegate other tasks to those who can handle them better.

Although outsourcing remains a critical element of the corporate strategic mix, success in today's complex outsourcing marketplace is contingent on new dynamics: specifically, the relationship between customer and service provider, according to a PricewaterhouseCoopers' global outsourcing study, "Outsourcing Comes of Age: The Rise of Collaborative Partnering.[1] The report says that cost savings is one of the drivers for outsourcing, in addition to several other benefits that outsourcing provides; these include access to

---

[1] PricewaterhouseCoopers, "Outsourcing Comes of Age: The Rise of Collaborative Partnering," 2008, www.pwc.com/en_gx/gx/operations-consulting-services/pdf/outsourcingcomesofage.pdf.

global capabilities such as human resources and talent, and physical resources. My personal experiences have been similar. Organizations outsource their IT operations for the following reasons:

- *To save money*: Cost savings are important, but this is only one of the reasons organizations outsource IT. Companies spend 80% of their IT budgets keeping the basic infrastructure running. That is dead money that does not contribute to growth. Most studies estimate 25% to 40% hard savings from outsourcing this work to a managed SPO, but SROs must understand and take into account the additional fees.

- *To improve company focus on core business practices*: Focusing on core business practices is the key to success for any organization that wants to grow in its business area. Organizations that are not IT SPOs do not need to spend time developing their IT skills but still need to use IT to manage and grow their businesses efficiently and effectively. Outsourcing IT aids in this situation.

- *To make capital funds available to aid in core business development*: Every business involves initial and ongoing investments, which every executive wants to invest in their core business rather than noncore businesses. Outsourcing IT enables organizations to spend their capital funds on items that are directly related to their business, products, and customers.

- *To reduce risk: for noncore business processes*. Keeping up with IT is essential for every IT company, and such tasks are expensive and time consuming. This is mandatory for organizations whose core business is IT; but for other organizations, it increases costs with less return on investment. Professional outsourced IT providers work with multiple clients and need to keep abreast of industry best practices, so they typically know what is right and what is not.

- *To access to the global IT talent pool across geographies:* Leaders looking beyond possible cost savings from outsourcing are also motivated by the quick availability of local talent to fulfill their project needs when they collaborate with an IT SPO. The concept of outsourcing has gained momentum because the model provides various benefits and enables organizations to access a broad base of skilled IT talent. This flexible staffing model for acquiring the right talent at the right time allows organizations to meet demand by quickly ramping up and ramping down resources, thereby providing timely and cost-effective solutions.

The Role of Governance in the Collaboration between IT Service Providers and Receivers

Governance of a SRO varies based on the size of the organization and the kind of business it performs; this is true especially for the company's core business. As an example, an organization in the manufacturing sector has core business departments that are quite different from those of a bank: the manufacturer has departments such as Production and Planning, Purchasing, Marketing, and Human Resources; the bank has departments such as Anti-money Laundering, Accounts, Investments, Loans, Banking Policy, Defaulters List, and Human Resource. Similarly, a retail organization specializing in consumer electronics organizes its core business departments differently than to a pharmaceutical company.

Although each industry is organized differently with respect to its core business, all organizations that outsource their IT business to an SPO organize their IT departments the same way. And every organization, regardless of industry, organizes and operates its governance in a similar fashion. Figure 5-1 depicts how the IT department of an SRO is organized in parallel to the governance of its IT SPO structure, which is quite different from the governance of an SRO's core business.

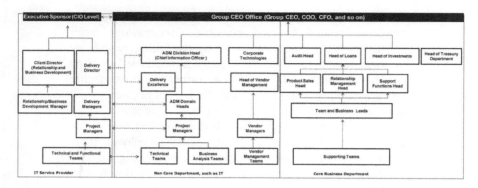

Figure 5-1. Governance of an IT SRO

In Figure 5-1, the right side represents the way a typical bank organizes its core business areas. This governance structure differs from organization to organization based on the business they perform.

The middle area, referred to as the *noncore department*, is the IT arm of the organization. It is led by a chief information officer (CIO) who is responsible for ensuring that all the core business entities of the organization are getting full support from the IT department, including development and maintenance of applications, managing the IT infrastructure, bringing new ideas in IT to enhance the user experience of clients, and so on.

Under every CIO, a person is responsible for each department of the IT function; these people are closely linked to and work with departments of the core business. For example, a banking organization may have functions such as a collateral management department and an asset service department; and each such department has a lead called the *domain head* or *department head*. The lead's responsibility is to ensure that IT support is provided to the core entities of the SRO for which that department is responsible. This support can be provided by in-house staff or SPOs. This role is also responsible for ensuring that the lead and the department's teams manage the SPOs to deliver outsourced contracts and manage relationships.

In an organization that outsources part of its IT work to SPOs, the CIO also has a direct line of reporting from the vendor manager, whose core function is to ensure that vendors deliver per their contracts and to measure the vendors' performance at periodic intervals. Another function that reports to the CIO is the delivery excellence function; this is an independent entity within the SRO's IT department that has the primary responsibility of assessing the quality of delivery by respective IT departments or domains. The head of vendor management reports to the CIO of the SRO; this person's duties involve managing the relationship with the SPO. Managing the vendor-management strategy includes but is not limited to managing the number of vendors, vendor risk management, and ensuring that the organization is getting the best from its vendors.

A project manager is responsible for ensuring that work is performed on schedule, within budget, and up to quality standards. This role works with in-house staff and an IT SPO team to deliver projects.

The governance of an IT SPO is always defined to match the governance of the IT SRO. As shown in Figure 5-1, the CIO level of the SPO maps to the agenda of the SRO group's CEO office overseeing IT needs. A client director and delivery director map to the CIO of the SRO; their job is to ensure that relationships and delivery, respectively, are managed to the customer's utmost satisfaction. Service provider delivery managers are responsible for delivering projects per the contract signed between the SPO and SRO; they map to the domain head of their respective domains. SPO project managers manage one or multiple projects that are to be delivered to the SRO. They are responsible for ensuring that projects are delivered per the contract, and they continually keep the SRO project managers informed about their projects' status.

As a rule, no organization outsources 100% of their IT business to an SPO. Companies want to manage the risk of vendor lock-in by retaining knowledge in-house.

Definition *Vendor lock-In* is a situation in which an SRO becomes fully dependent on an SPO (also referred to as a *vendor*) for products and services. In such a situation, the SRO does not possess the required knowledge to perform the work in-house and cannot transition to another SPO.

Vendor lock-in carries huge risks because the organization must deal with the ups and downs of its IT service provider with no choice of switching to in-house development or choosing another SPO. My experiences working with several SROs have demonstrated that a company can manage the risk of vendor lock-in if it takes the following actions:

- Performs at least 20% to 30% of IT services work in-house

- Enables its staff to spread themselves across all applications and services that vendors are working on such that knowledge is acquired regarding the outsourced work

- Fills key positions in outsourced projects such as technical and application architects, business architects, lead designers, and lead developers

In this model, in-house staff members typically obtain required technical and business knowledge about applications that SPOs are using. With little effort, they can take over work from SPOs or transfer work to a new SPO, when required.

Key Points

- Organizations with an IT budget of more than $1 billion USD year on year are categorized as Tier-1 IT SROs.

- Organizations with an IT budget in the range from $200 million USD to $1 billion USD year on year are categorized as Tier-2 IT SROs.

- Organizations with an IT budget of less than $200 million USD year on year are categorized as Tier-3 IT SROs.

- Organizations outsource their IT operations to achieve cost savings, improve company focus on core business practices, make capital funds available to aid in core business development, reduce risk from noncore business processes, and enable access to the global IT talent pool across geographies.

- Vendor lock-in is a situation in which a SRO becomes fully dependent on an SPO (also referred to as a vendor) for products and services.

- As a rule, no organization outsources 100% of its IT business to an SPO, because it wants to manage the risk of vendor lock-in by retaining knowledge in-house.

CHAPTER

6

Selecting Your IT Service Provider

The IT function continues to be asked to handle more demand for services in the face of growing technological complexity. Pressure on IT will persist as IT SROs are faced with flat or shrinking IT budgets and at the same time are expected to develop IT to create business value and innovation. This pressure is transferred to the SPOs, because they often become the IT arms of the associated SROs.

As a result, organizations of all sizes are examining their strategies to determine whether the IT services they are designing and delivering both via in-house mechanisms and with their IT SPOs can be made more efficient and effective. The Meta Group, an analyst of the IT outsourcing industry, in 2003 estimated that 70% of companies were outsourcing and that all companies would adopt the outsourcing model by 2006.[1] This indicates that CIOs who are focused on growth will partner with IT SPOs to obtain new skills and expertise rather than conduct these functions in-house. Further, they are trying to move away from traditional IT SPOs that provide "vanilla" services and are not sufficiently innovative to bring value to the SRO. Increasingly, IT organizations are looking to trusted IT SPOs to help reduce costs, manage complexity, maintain leading-edge skills, and adopt technological innovations.

Negotiating the lowest possible price for these services is no longer sufficient and is not beneficial to either the SPO or the SRO. SROs need to demand more. They need business advice, guidance, and expertise to manage their IT

---

[1]"We'll All Be Outsourcing by 2006," *Computing*, July 10, 2003.

landscape. They require an organization that focuses less on price and more on value. SPOs that focus on these core priorities will achieve sustainable growth in the future.

Traditionally, SROs have tended to select SPOs that are appropriate for the size of the SRO, with some exceptions. As an example, Tier-1 SROs tend to engage Tier-1 SPOs and sometimes Tier-2 SPOs for their IT business. Tier-2 SROs partner with Tier-2 SPOs, and so on. However, in the current business environment, size is not the only criterion necessary for selecting an appropriate SPO.

Some organizations choose to continue their relationships with existing SPOs because of legacy relationships, even though the value provided by such SPOs is not may not be on par with their competitors. These SROs are risk-averse and leery of making changes, although there may be benefits related to making such a switch.

The Right Service Provider for Your Business

In simple terms, the right SPO is the one that constantly strives to invest in its employees to remain ahead of the technology curve, that is in line with market changes, and that employs these advancements to its customers' benefit via its employees. Such organizations have established a trademark in the IT services industry as being innovative companies that are huge assets to their customers.

However, many such organizations are able to maintain these reputations only until they have reached a certain growth level. Following that point, like some of their inferior peers, they lose the spirit of bringing innovative ideas to their customers, because growth has become their core focus. I have known organizations that have moved to Tier-1 status from Tier-3 in just a few years because of their strong reputation as innovative companies when they were Tier-3. But as soon as they became Tier-1 companies, they lost the charisma of innovation. Although the strategy for such an organization—being an innovative company—remains the same, translating that organizational strategy to each and every employee is unmanageable due to the scale of the company's growth. Such an organization is not a sound long-term choice, and SROs should accordingly to a more appropriate SPO as soon as possible.

The right partner is one that is not just delivering high-quality services at a better cost, but that is also constantly generating and implementing ideas to reduce the total cost of ownership to the SRO. Innovation is the core of this arrangement, in addition to several other influencing factors. This section discusses some areas that SROs tend not to consider when selecting an IT SPO. There are some other areas that are commonly emphasized but that are not discussed in this section, including the SPO's experience in relevant areas, security considerations, the solution matching the requirements, a focus on low and competitive pricing, references from other customers, commitments made by the SPO, experience with global delivery models, consistent processes, and knowledge management and SPO certifications; a wide range of literature dating from 1970–2014 is already available concerning the selection of SPOs using these emphases.

Assessing a Provider's Flexibility and Innovative Capability

Many books address the adoption of innovation, but rarely discussed is what an SRO should expect from an SPO in tangible terms with respect to innovation. *Innovation*, in my terminology, involves gathering all relevant services from an SPO for the benefit of the SRO. Innovation summons the full potential of the SPO as a whole and puts it at the disposal of the SPO's customers. In my experience, I have won, retained, and grown business with numerous customers; this was possible only by bringing continuous value to my customers with new ideas and innovations. An SRO needs to understand the method by which an SPO promises to bring value to it, and at what cost. For me, supplying the full capabilities of the SPO via innovation is not a separate service with an associated cost, but is rather part of the job for any SPO. To ensure that such a service can be realized by the SPO, an SRO must be made aware of the existing practices and services the SPO offers, and must understand the methodology by which these services will be brought to the SRO's benefit by the SPO. A mechanism under which the total cost of ownership will be measured in tangible terms should be defined by the SPO. The depth and breadth of the services should be assessed thoroughly before making a decision. Let me explain this with a case study.

Client Profile: Leading Bank

Client name: RMG Corporation

Size: 50,000 employees

This case study involves RMG Corporation, with whom we conducted business along with two major competitors for several years. We had been competing with each other and trying to break into each other's contracts, and some of my competitors were even successful in breaking a few of them.

Although I do not shy away from competing with peer organizations, my major focus at RMG Corporation was to create my own market space and fill a unique role for my customer by identifying solutions that could bring value to the customer business and the IT landscape. I wanted to keep myself separate from my competitors in at least some areas. This was possible only by understanding my customer's challenges and analyzing RMG's competitive landscape against its peers. Once this understanding was achieved, I was able to bring services from my organization that overcame the challenges and made RMG more competitive in its market space.

I consider this approach the attainment of success. In addition to creating untapped business potential for myself, I also gained customer confidence as an innovative service provider who considered customer growth and challenges. This was achieved by employing all of my relevant organizational services for the benefit of the customer. I created a framework around innovation after coming to understand the full capabilities of my organization in each horizontal. I did this by analyzing my customer's challenges, short-term goals, and long-term and market strategies and competition, in concert with my teams.

I began to propose ideas that would benefit the customer. This was a continuous process over the course of the relationship, and year-on-year we were able to save the customer several million dollars with these services. Not only were we able to increase our business share with this customer, but we were also the organization regarded as their most trusted advisor.

Matching Provider Offerings with Receiver Goals

I discussed in Chapter 2 that each organization has a unique differentiator that identifies versus its competitors. Some organizations differentiate themselves with a cultural match, some with superior client-facing skills, some with superior business-domain skills, and others with high employee availability in developing or developed countries. An SRO needs to understand the strengths of each SPO in order to effectively select a new SPO or to continue a relationship with an existing SPO, because the company will achieve quality output and meet its goals based on these strengths.

As an example, suppose Tier-1 Multinational Service Provider Company A has a huge employee base in Europe, featuring local talent, and prides itself on being the company that has the best cultural match to European society. Several European SROs with various classifications (Tier-1, Tier-2, and Tier-3) are worried about engaging an international SPO due to the fear of cultural mismatch. Although the goal is to outsource their IT business, they still want to retain the local culture because they understand that their employees are immersed in that culture and lack experience working with international teams. These organizations want to ensure that they do not create cultural barriers at work and that employees work at the same level of productivity even after their company engages an IT SPO. For such an organization, Tier-1 Multinational Service Provider Company A will rate positively when compared with other SPOs in the selection process, due to its employee strength regarding local culture.

Another example is a Tier-1 pure player SPO named Company B, which has a huge employee base in developing countries. SRO B is seeking to create a new application over a short time period but at low cost, which requires an immediate and large-scale ramp-up of highly skilled IT staff. Employees of Company B are highly experienced in working with international teams.

Company B can score extra points in the SRO's selection process because it has employees who are experienced in dealing with international cultures. It also has a proven capability to ramp up a large number of teams within a short duration, because it maintains a large bench in low-cost countries.

Finally, consider Tier-2 SPO Company C, which provides unique services in cloud computing. The company services customers for this technology area exclusively. Company C will score extra points with SROs that are seeking services in cloud computing.

Evaluating a Provider's Financial Stability

Whether you are considering a relatively short-term relationship with an SPO or a long-term association, the financial stability of the IT SPO is of utmost importance to consider when engaging with such a provider. An IT SPO's length of stay in the marketplace and its size are not useful measures for predicting its reliability and sustainability. I know of several instances in which Tier-1 SPOs became entangled in legal litigation that impacted their services to their customers. In evaluating SPOs, an SRO should validate annual reports, financial statements, and opinions offered by business and IT industry press and analysts, along with customer references and quantified success metrics.

Discovering a Provider's Employee Attrition Rate

Attrition can be detrimental both to a business's bottom line and to the quality of service provided to customers. Currently, the average attrition levels across the IT industry vary from 10% to 12%, as discussed in Chapter 4.

An SRO needs to carefully understand this percentage—not at the organizational level but for the unit of the SPO that will be delivering services to the SRO—to accurately predict the quality of service continuity from this SPO. After all, the IT business is employee intensive, and the success of IT services depends on human resources.

Detailing a Provider's Access to Skills and Human Resources

Many IT SPOs exist in the industry, and nearly all of them claim to have a large number of human resource skills available based on the size of the organization and needs of an SRO. I have encountered several SPOs that claimed to maintain a large-percentage resource bench and to be able to deploy the required numbers on projects in just a few days.

Although this may not be a false claim from many SPOs, the most essential part for an SRO to understand is how to assess bench resources based on the employees' experience level. My experience says that 80% of bench resources are fresh college graduates who have almost no experience with working on projects and who may not be candidates who can fit the SRO's needs on a short-term basis. Before making a selection, an SRO needs to map the SPO's human resource availability and the experience level of those human resources to the human resource needs of the SRO's IT business.

Conclusions

In an age of booming technology, running a business without IT is impossible. Technology has become an integral part of the way business is done, and almost all organizations have achieved growth only by taking advantage of IT. Even if an organization performs services or provides products that are not technology-related in and of themselves, such as manufacturing cars or selling products in a store, without an information management system, it is next to impossible to do business and grow in today's world.

Having the right IT SPO has therefore become one of the essential elements for the success of any SRO, because the success or failure of a business is now fully dependent on IT. An SPO that can bring innovation to the SRO, thereby helping the organization to perform its business in a much more efficient way and increase customer satisfaction, is one that will experience long-term growth. This discussion not only applies to selecting a new SPO, but also includes guiding factors to be validated by any SRO for its existing SPOs.

Key Points

- The right SPO is the one that constantly strives to invest in its employees to remain ahead of the technology curve, that is in line with market changes, and that employs these advancements to its customers' benefit via its employees.

- Innovation involves gathering all relevant services from an SPO for the benefit of the SRO.

- An SRO needs to understand the strengths of each SPO in order to effectively select a new SPO or to continue a relationship with an existing SPO, because the company will achieve quality output and meet its goals based on these strengths.

- Whether you are considering a relatively short-term relationship with a SPO or a long-term association, the financial stability of an IT SPO is of utmost importance to consider when engaging with such a provider.

- An SRO needs to carefully understand the attrition percentage not at the organizational level but for the unit of the SPO that will be delivering services to the SRO, to accurately predict the quality of service continuity from this SPO.

- Before making a selection, an SRO needs to map the SPO's human resource availability and the experience level of the SPO's human resources to the human resource needs of the SRO's IT business.

Understanding Your IT Service Provider

Several studies have found that SPOs need to know and understand their customers to better serve those customers. There is a difference between knowing who the customer is and understanding the customer. *Knowing* the customers typically means identifying who they are demographically, assessing what content they are reading and what business they do, and so on. *Understanding* the customer means knowing their interests, problems, objectives, governance, business and people behaviors and preferences, why and when they buy a service, how they buy, how much money they have, and what they think about you and your competition. I know of several SPOs that address these topics effectively because their goal is to increase their business and to gain a larger IT market share. They do everything required to make this happen.

The more an SPO understands its customers, the more effective its sales and marketing efforts can be. Hence, effective SPOs attempt to determine

- What a specific customer purchases
- Why they buy it

Although not discussed widely, knowing and understanding an SPO carries the same importance for the SRO. Most companies do a good job of knowing their SPOs because it is relatively easy to do so by reading about the SPO's demographics, what the SPO does, and so on. To understand the SPO's strengths,

SROs rely on a few resources such as the sales or delivery personnel of the SPO who interact with them on a regular basis. However, many SROs fail to understand their SPOs fully, which entails identifying the strengths of the SPO as well as its weaknesses, its governance, the technological realms in which it is expert, and areas in which it is investing and developing its employee strengths. It is essential for an SRO to fully understand its SPO in order to extract maximum benefits from the SPO. Otherwise, the SRO is dependent on a set of people from the SPO for an understanding of the SPO's full potential; and in most cases, this complex subject cannot to fully understood by consulting only a few sources. Understanding the IT SPO is essential in order for the SRO to unleash the SPO's full potential.

Know Your IT Service Provider

An SRO needs to be aware of several angles before engaging with an SPO as well as during the tenure of a relationship with the SPO. This will enable personnel from the SRO to extract the full potential of its SPOs, in addition to defining strategies that can enable consistent quality output from the SPOs. Knowing the SPO also helps to achieve an understanding of its organizational challenges and risks, based on which risk-mitigation strategies can be devised. This is one of the critical elements in today's demanding market space, in which a significant level of effort is required from the SRO to understand their SPOs that will assure them that they will receive the desired quality service from their SPOs. SRO.

Governance Structure and Personnel

It is important to understand the governance of the SPO in terms of its organizational structure: who reports to whom, their horizontals, and services offered within these horizontals. Understanding the horizontal structure is essential, because these subject matter units in an SPO can bring enormous value to customer businesses: horizontals are created with the aim of bringing the latest and most relevant technology to solve business problems and propel customer businesses forward. Horizontals continually incubate new approaches and service offerings to prepare clients for new technologies with significant business potential. They focus on technologies and services that promise to reduce costs, streamline processes, and speed time-to-market.

The reason to understand the SPO's organizational governance is that an SRO should be able to reach the right people at the right time to accomplish its goals. Some SPOs, while defining governance for their customer business, limit themselves by establishing a line of hierarchy or reporting structure without understanding the fact that governance means more than that: it is a tool, using which the SRO can achieve the full results it expects from its SPOs.

Horizontals and Services

Organizations want to focus on their core business while outsourcing their non-core activities—in this case, IT—to an SPO whose core business is IT. Organizations do not invest heavily in areas that do not make up their core business. Based on this concept, every SRO expects the best possible IT service from its IT SPO.

The main objective of the IT staff in an SRO is to ensure that they are aware of the SPO horizontals that relate most closely to their business, and the IT landscape that can add value to their core business. A step further is to understand the different services offered by these horizontals and how those services can bring business benefits to the SRO. The only way the SRO can achieve such an understanding is by mandating that the SPO create an approach based on which such offerings can be made available to the SRO.

Typically, it is the job of an SPO to constantly bring new ideas via its horizontals to improve the performance of its customer businesses. However, such a service is not guaranteed with most SPOs, because it depends on the person or people from the SRO with whom the SPO's staff interacts—and few people are motivated to bring such value to the customer. Hence, it is imperative for an SRO to mandate the creation of an approach that enables knowledge flow regarding service; this is referred to as a *Consultative Selling Framework* (CSF). A CSF is built on the core value of the SPO bringing ideas to the SRO that can benefit the SRO via the SPO's horizontals and different entities within the SPO.

Center of Excellence

Centers of excellence (COEs) are departments within an SPO that focus on specific areas, searching both inside and outside the organization to capture new knowledge and practices. Increasingly, SPOs are focusing more on these COEs, and new technologies that emerge in the market tend to be prototyped here, including the creation of tools that can help bring value to the customer.

A COE comprises a functional or cross-functional team set up as a physical or virtual team, but it has permanent rather than just project status. It is essential for an SRO to stay current with events in COEs that closely relate to its business, to become familiar with industry trends, and to survey the competitive landscape. It is also essential to define an approach by which tools created by the COE that closely relate to the SRO technology landscape are validated and adopted at regular intervals. Organizations invest in the most valuable projects and create economies of scale for their service offerings via their COEs. Similar to understanding the horizontals of SPOs, understanding COEs that closely relate to the SRO's business and IT landscape is essential, and this can be achieved by mandating that the SRO create an approach that enables knowledge flow regarding services.

Market Intelligence and Trends

Market intelligence is information relevant to a company's markets, gathered and analyzed specifically for the purpose of accurate and confident decision-making when determining strategy in areas such as market opportunity, market penetration strategy, and market development. Most IT SPO companies invest in understanding the market situation for each and every vertical or business domain in which their customers have a presence. Based on this data, SPOs try to identify potential new clients and opportunities for business, as well as to make individuals from their organization aware of trends specific to their customers' business. This provides their employees a leading edge to speak the customers' language and to confer with customers about the way the customers' industry is evolving.

Each SRO has its own market intelligence wing, which may be strong but is focused on the core business domain. In most such organizations, this department provides minimal information about technology advancements in the market space because IT is not the company's core business. To compensate for this gap, it is essential to take advantage of the full benefits of the SPO's market intelligence division in the SRO's specific line of business.

Interpreting Company Results

Each SRO must understand its IT requirements, based on which it can define a strategy for selecting the right SPO. It is essential to understand the SPO's key company results. Some areas of focus include how a specific SPO manages its resource bench, such as its utilization ratio (including trainees/freshers and excluding trainees/freshers), cost structures, profit margins, and employee attrition levels. Several conclusions can be derived from these parameters that will help an SRO to make strategic decisions with respect to the selection and management of an SPO.

For example, a Tier-1 company with very high utilization ratio of more than 95% (excluding trainees/freshers) may pose a risk to the SRO if the business foresees a large and sudden ramp-up of resources. In this case, a risk-mitigation plan needs to be requested from the SPO. A similar example involves an organization with an average utilization ratio of 90%–95% excluding trainees/freshers and an average utilization ratio of 65%–70% including trainees/freshers. The interpretation of this data could be that for any given resource needs, a large number of freshers could be deployed to projects; the SRO needs to carefully define a strategy that will enable the SPO to deploy skilled resources to projects. The SRO must validate the resource-loading strategy that the SPO will adopt for project execution.

Another example is to look at the SPO's employee attrition levels, which have a direct impact on the SPO's quality of service. Because IT is highly dependent on skilled and knowledgeable resources, a high attrition rate may entail the loss of knowledge from the SPO, which may lead to low-quality service or inconsistent output quality. Predictability of the quality of service provided is of utmost importance in the IT industry.

Key Points

- Centers of excellence are departments that focus on specific areas, searching both inside and outside the organization to capture new knowledge and practices.

- Market intelligence is information relevant to a company's markets, gathered and analyzed specifically for the purpose of accurate and confident decision-making when determining strategy in areas such as market opportunity, market penetration strategy, and market development.

- The SRO's IT staff should understand the governance of the SPO in terms of its organizational structure: who reports to whom, their horizontals, and services offered within those horizontals.

- The SRO's IT staff should be aware of the SPO horizontals that closely relate to the SRO's business and IT landscape and that can add value to the core business.

- The SRO's IT staff need to understand the SPO's COE departments that closely relate to the SRO's business and IT landscape.

- To understand IT advancements, it is essential for an SRO to take advantage of the full benefits from its SPO's market intelligence division in the specific line of business.

- It is essential for the SRO IT staff to understand the SPO's key company results, with specific focus on the resource bench, cost structures, profit margins, and employee attrition.

Mapping and Managing Your Service Providers

All of us want to be part of a winning team. In a running competition, the gold medalist may have beaten the silver medalist by a mere 0.001 of a second, but we, the great majority of the viewers, treat the gold medalist as the differentiator in the class. Here, the winner's confidence and hard work make the difference. In contrast, a soccer team achieves success by the entire team performing with the winning spirit and representing a winning agenda. If anyone on the team fails to perform, the entire team loses. Only a motivated and skilled individual can be a winner, displaying the winning spirit to others and inspiring the entire team to win.

In today's world, which emphasizes doing more with less and working "smarter, not harder," teamwork is more important than ever. No group of people or individuals working in isolation can do better than several key individuals working together can. In fact, one definition of a winning team is one in which "the whole is greater than the sum of the parts." Synergy is essential but elusive. The best team attracts the best people.

In the software industry, success is always centered on people and resources. It is not about knowing how to write code, but about knowing and analyzing how to create a better software product. I have personally experienced that it is better to have motivated, actuated, and skilled people on the team, communicating and working toward the goal using minimal processes (that is, processes that are useful for the project) than to have a well-defined process used by unmotivated individuals.

This is the relationship that must be shared between employees from an SPO and an SRO. Excellence cannot be achieved merely by the SRO desiring it. Employees from both the SPO and the SRO should collaborate and exert comparable effort to understand each other and ensure that service delivery is achieved with high quality. Project excellence is achieved when the project stakeholders, including the project teams, all commit to the common goal and work together to make it happen. Hence, it is imperative for the SRO to understand the SPO before starting to manage it, to achieve exceptional results. This is the true meaning of a partnership between an SPO and an SRO.

Managing Your Service Provider

Value for money (VFM) is a term used to assess whether an organization has obtained the maximum potential benefit from the goods and services received from its SPOs. Achieving maximum benefit is a very subjective assessment: in the traditional model, delivering what has been agreed on in the contract signed by the SRO and the SPO is considered "getting maximum benefit." However, in the current business environment, delivering what has been agreed on in the contract is considered merely standard.

Attaining maximum benefit is achieved only by extracting the full potential from the SPO and is not limited to the formal contract. To achieve this, you must manage your SPO in the most efficient way to receive full benefits from its expertise. This means the SRO also needs to support the SPO to achieve the contractual and non-contractual goals set by the SRO; doing so encourages full collaboration and trust between the parties.

Chapter 7 discussed how SROs need to fully understand their SPOs. Understanding the strengths and weaknesses of SPOs can help SROs define an engagement model to manage the SPOs in the most efficient way by doing the following:

- Utilizing the strengths of the SPO to improve the IT landscape. Employing these strengths in an efficient way can help SROs to stay ahead of the technology curve with respect to competitors, resulting in reduced costs, innovation, and better value for the money spent.

- Monitoring the SPO to ensure that current weaknesses do not affect the SRO. Creating risk-mitigation plans is also useful to manage weaknesses that may directly or indirectly impact the SRO.

Networking

Once you engage an IT SPO to perform IT work for you, it becomes essential to treat the people of the organization as part of your team. Similar to the way personnel from the SPO try their best to foster networking in the SRO, it is essential for the SRO to have the right contacts with the SPO. Although the underlying agenda for networking is different for each of these organizations, there are benefits for both.

It is essential to recognize the key people in the SPO (including individuals from horizontals, CEOs, and marketing intelligence), their roles and responsibilities, and how can they contribute to the governance defined between the SPO and the SRO. I have encountered several cases in which my customers were able to solve issues that were treated as impossible by people from the SPO who worked with them closely. Networking lets you reach the right people at the right time to solve issues beyond the scope of the few employees from the SPO with whom the SRO may interact.

An SRO needs to mandate that the SPO keep it updated on any organizational changes and key developments within the SPO.

Organization Entity Awareness

I have discussed that an SRO needs to understand the full structure of the SPO. This entails first understanding the overall organizational structure and its entities and then focusing on those entities within the SRO that closely relate to the SRO's business and IT landscape and that can add value to its core business, directly or indirectly. A few such areas include horizontals and the services within them, centers of excellence (COEs) and their expertise, and the market intelligence function. It is essential to ask the SPO to keep the SRO regularly posted about changes and developments in these areas, which can often be used to the SRO's benefit.

Let me explain with a case study about how one of my customers achieved maximum benefit from its SPO by using this model.

Client Profile: Leading bank in the United States

Client Name: ABC Financials

Size: 200,000 employees

ABC Financials is considered one of the top innovative banks in the United States, primarily because it is the foremost bank to implement cutting-edge technologies that enable optimal customer experiences:

- It was one of the first institutions to implement mobile banking.

- It was one of a few to implement eWallet, which is a mobile money-transfer solution for users of smartphones and tablet computer devices.

- It was the first to employ strategies using the email-based payment systems Bitcoin and TransferWise.

How has it been possible for ABC Financials to lead in the market and to be known as a top innovative bank?

For decades, ABC Financials has been outsourcing 70% of its IT business to SPOs, and it manages its SPOs similarly to its internal staff. This does not mean ABC Financials is an easygoing customer for its SPOs. The strategy of ABC Financials is to understand each and every SPO fully, in order to manage them well and to extract their full potential. ABC Financials achieves this by enabling its staff to understand the different entities within the SPOs.

ABC Financials made an effort to understand these various entities and then selected several of the entities that closely related to its business and IT landscape. Some examples were the cloud horizontal, the mobile banking horizontal, the business intelligence division, the application rationalization division, the market and intelligence wing for the credit cards domain, the market and intelligence wing for the retail banking domain, related CEOs, and entities developing Intellectual properties in the banking domain.

The SPOs were informed a framework agreement called an *innovation contract* had been developed, mandating that they bring new ideas to ABC Financials. The innovation contract specified that at least 20 new ideas per year must be shared with ABC Financials that could add value to the core business; 50% of those ideas would need to be considered by ABC Financials sufficiently innovative for implementation. A financial target was assigned to this contract. ABC Financials maintained equal rigor by identifying leads who could help validate the ideas shared by the SPOs.

Each SPO created a methodology, using which different entities in the organizations started to share new ideas via newsletter twice a month about existing services and new services and their benefits, including case studies. The market intelligence divisions were engaged to keep ABC Financials updated on market trends in the credit cards domain. A few personnel from the SRO were made accountable for delving deep into services that could benefit the business, and a few were made accountable for researching market trends made available by the SPOs. The intellectual properties, tools, and techniques created by the SPOs were validated at frequent intervals, and those that would benefit the SRO were selected for implementation.

This was all achieved by establishing a well-defined process around innovation. Detailing this process, however, is outside the scope of this book. Although the process appears time-consuming on paper, its takes only a few minutes per week for SRO personnel to achieve the substantial benefits that come from employing this model.

Based on this model, ABC Financials was able to generate 60% of its innovations directly from its SPOs. For example, ABC Financials took advantage of the Application Portfolio rationalization service from Service Provider A, which reduced its overall IT spending by 15%. In another case, based on data shared by the market intelligence division of Service Provider B, ABC Financials presented its research on eWallet to few of their customers and asked them if they will be interested to have eWallet as one of the addition service from ABC Financials. The feedback was very positive, and based on this, ABC Financials implemented eWallet as part of their new service offering, which gained much traction in the market after its implementation.

Every SRO needs to verify that an efficient engine is in place to ensure the proper flow of services from each of its SPOs

Optimizing Outcomes in Terms of Cost, Schedule, and Quality Variables

The most difficult challenge for any organization to address involves effort slippages, which often have a direct impact on costs. *Effort slippage* means the actual effort to execute a project is higher than estimated.

Another facet that personnel from SROs need to address involves negotiating contract specifications for effort, because reducing effort directly provides cost advantages. I have encountered a few customers who are very tough negotiators and sometimes unrealistic when negotiating about the effort required for their project's execution. I have heard from some of my teams after such debates, "They are our customers, so we need to accept what they say; otherwise we lose our relationship." I have also heard, "Even though they are our customers, we cannot agree to their estimates because of these 10 reasons, and we need to convince them somehow." I am always supportive of the latter response, for two reasons:

- All negotiated business should be mutually beneficial, and no one should sign a business deal that will not yield profits for them.

- Given unrealistic agreements concerning effort, effort slippages are bound to occur.

Some customers try to maintain their focus on effort estimations for any project and want to pay the lowest possible fees to their SPOs without understanding the consequence of this strategy. Every business needs to be profitable, and in these cases everyone makes their best efforts to achieve profitability in any given scenario. For example, in cases involving unrealistic effort estimates, I have seen SPO managers ask their teams to stretch beyond normal working hours to achieve on-time and on-cost delivery. A workday might run from 8 hours to as much as 24 hours. Another trick is to compromise on the number of reviews of deliverables, which has a direct impact on the quality of work. There can even be instances where testing time is reduced to achieve financial targets.

I don't blame the SPOs for their actions in such cases. An SRO should understand that cost benefits can be achieved in ways other than effort reduction. Effort reduction is not a good area to repeatedly negotiate. Too many unrealistic negotiations can lead to employee burnout and reduced quality of work products, neither of which is beneficial to the SRO.

In most organizations, the legacy is that management addresses the financial targets, and the technical and functional teams have targets concerning delivery timelines and quality. This is an efficient distribution of responsibilities. Instead of SROs focusing too much on effort reduction, they should focus on cost reduction. Different methods can be applied to achieve this, such as requesting discounts on rates of resources that will be assigned by SPO to work for SRO , discounts on rates if a certain volume of work is assigned to the SPO, and other means. As a result, the teams working on projects are motivated to continue working for the same SRO because they have a good work-life balance and a healthy working relationship. This ensure the quality and on-time delivery of their products.

Let me explain with a case study about a customer that tried to achieve cost benefits from their SPOs by choosing to focus heavily on effort reduction but ultimately failed to achieve the desired results.

Client Profile: Leading retail company in London

Client Name: CZ Corporation

Size: 18,000 employees

CZ Corporation is a small but well-known consumer electronics company headquartered in London. Personnel from its IT department are widely recognized for being a group of "tough customers" who extract the best out of their IT SPOs. They also reward their SPOs when exceptional results are achieved; in several cases, SPOs have been rewarded with financial incentives.

CZ Corporation is highly cost focused. Although not every employee is trained for this purpose, each and every employee of the IT division attempts to get the best work out of their SPOs by using effort reduction as a lever.

One large IT multinational SPO and three Tier-2 SPOs were managing CZ Corporation's IT business. CZ Corporation used its negotiation and pressure skills to reduce the effort estimations presented by the SPO teams. After just two years, CZ Corporation realized that the attrition in its SPO teams had reached 30%, compared to an organization and industry average of 10% to 12%. Several projects were delivered with low quality and schedule slippages. Effort estimates were directly influencing project schedules: SPOs could not add safety time to project baseline schedules to guarantee a high probability of timely completion. After several projects encountered a similar situation, the CIO of CZ Corporation became worried. A very brief analysis revealed that the tough, unrealistic negotiations regarding project effort caused the SPOs to burn their employees with long work hours and weekend work, to try to ensure that they were profitable and that delivery was on-time.

After a few months, the teams on the ground became frustrated, and almost all of them were looking for opportunities to cease working for CZ Corporation. Many even left their employing organization rather than continuing to work for CZ Corporation. This included management staff. These problems made the team unstable, and average application knowledge diminished on the SPO teams, which led to low-quality output and schedule slippages. For example, Person A, who spent 2 years working for CZ Corporation, was able to accomplish a segment of project development in 1 day, whereas the same work required 3 days for Person B, who joined the team only 3 months previously. This was due to the knowledge gap between these two employees. One of the SPOs achieved a negative profit margin continuously for 2 years while working with CZ Corporation. Ultimately, the CEO of this SPO asked his executive teams why they should not walk away from doing further business from CZ Corporation.

Although this was a very extreme case, it indicates the risk that an SRO carries when its staff tries to achieve cost advantages with unrealistic effort estimates and schedule demands. Such strategies soon backfire and result in project disasters impacting the core business.

In summary, the key to success with IT SPOs is to focus on keeping at least the employees in the middle and at the bottom of the pyramid happy and motivated; this requires better management of the lower pyramid even though there can be pressure on individuals at the top. One way to achieve this is by providing enough time for teams to complete their tasks.

Human Resource Management

Many SROs recognize and reward individuals from SPOs who are on par with their own employees. However, most organizations in the current business environment work with their SPOs in distributed environments, where much of the teams is located remotely. It is always difficult to assess the potential of people situated at remote locations, but it is essential for staff from the SRO to go the extra mile to communicate with motivated individuals across geographies. Even a few words of appreciation from a customer can have a big impact on an individual, and it is a human tendency to thrive on praise. With such motivation, employees will aspire to continue working with the same customers for the long term. This benefits SROs, because knowledge is preserved and builds over a period of time, resulting in increased quality of work.

I have encountered several customers who aspire to keep their teams happy by recognizing them, including the staff of their SPOs. But in most cases, this recognition is limited to staff in client-facing roles, because these are the individuals who interact with the customers on a daily basis; thus it is easy to identify high performers. In today's world, where team members are often located remotely in developing countries, especially in the offshoring world, it is essential that personnel from the SRO maintain a close connection globally and ensure that their key resources are recognized and rewarded regardless of their location.

AB Securities is a large bank based out of Japan. We were its IT SPO, operating in a global delivery model with more than 100 people working from AB Securities' site in India. AB Securities understands that people are its assets, and to secure long-term success, it has to manage its human resources so they are happy. To achieve this, the company adopted the following strategy:

1. All senior staff of AB Securities are required to visit India at least once a year.

2. Different awards were designed to recognize employees and were presented by the staff of AB Securities during their visits to India. Some awards were presented in person by the CIO.

3. The senior executive made a phone call to ground-level staff whenever there was a significant accomplishment or exceptional work was done by an employee.

4. A portion of the money resulting from the contract signed between the SPO and AB Securities was set aside to reward high-performing teams and individuals (for example, they were awarded music players, given time off on international holidays, and so on).

5. The company welcomed innovative ideas for improving AB Securities from all team members and rewarded the best innovation.

Keeping the morale of the team working for you at a high level is one of the key success factors for any organization, regardless of whether these employees are your own staff or come from an SPO.

It is also essential for any SRO to identify the key resources from its SPOs. Key resources are those who are important for achieving project success based on their performance, experience level, and knowledge of the SRO's business and applications. Typically, this involves categorizing 20% to 30% of the SPO staff in roles such as project managers, technical and business architects, lead developers, and designers.

Based on this concept, AB Securities implemented two measures:

- Contractual agreement with the SPO to create a core team consisting of 40% of the staff working for AB Securities. The contract carries a financial target. The service-level agreement (SLA) with the SPO is intended to limit attrition on the core team to 5%, which is measured at the end of each year. Attrition greater than 5% carries a financial penalty, and attrition less than 5% entails a bonus.

- Contractual agreement that the SPO provides a bonus to the core team each year.

The key to success for any business is retaining top talent and continuously motivating them.

Managing Attrition and Targets

Going the extra mile and keeping teams motivated is a good practice for SROs to follow, but it is essential that attrition be measured and that targets be defined for SPOs. The average standards for attrition are 10% to 12%, which can be considered normal. However, the SRO must establish reasonable attrition levels for the whole team and the core team and agree on them with the SPO.

Although it is essential for the SRO to understand trends in the attrition levels of its SPO companies, at the same time the SRO needs to define a target attrition value for the SPO within its span of business with the SPO. However, a good SPO shows results and manages attrition at the organizational level.

There is a chance that the target percentage will not be achieved by the human resources deployed by the SPO for the specific SRO business. If attrition is high, it often leads to lost knowledge and low product quality. In the previous case study, AB Securities defined an attrition target for its SPO. CZ Corporation went a step further and defined a SLA not only with respect to the core teams but also for the SPO's entire set of teams.

Client Profile: Leading retail company in London

Client name: CZ Corporation

Size: 18,000 employees

As already discussed, CZ Corporation is a consumer electronics corporation headquartered in London having multiple SPOs such as Company A and Company B. During the start of the relationship with its SPOs, CZ Corporation did not realize that it would have to measure the attrition of its SPOs to ensure knowledge retention, which is the backbone of quality product delivery by the SPOs. In year 1, due to high attrition from Company B, missed deadlines and several project defects ultimately led to business users' dissatisfaction. Understanding the importance of retaining employees for continued quality service, in year 2, CZ Corporation mandated all their service providers to measure attrition and publish results on attrition to them.

Company A, published their results, which had an organizational-level attrition rate of 13% and a CZ Corporation–level attrition rate of 11% for year 2. CZ Corporation–level attrition indicates attrition among the human resources deployed by Company A for the work and tenure of the contract defined between CZ Corporation and Company A. Company B is another SPO for CZ Corporation that had an organizational-level attrition of 8% and account-level attrition of 19.8% for year 2.

After analyzing the attrition results of its SPOs, CZ Corporation defined attrition targets for each and every SPO based on the following:

- 10% attrition target for all SPO resources deployed on CZ Corporation projects.

- 5% attrition target year on year for the core team. The core team, in the context of CZ Corporation, was defined as 40% of the SPO resources working for the company, selected based on performance, type of work, and location.

The attrition targets defined by CZ Corporation had a direct financial consequence for their SPOs. If an SPO was able to keep attrition at less than 2% for the core team, a bonus was announced by CZ Corporation, similar to the case study involving AB Securities.

Attrition management is an important issue in any industry today and is particularly essential for the IT industry because it is a technologically savvy industry that is entirely dependent on its employees. Various estimates from insiders place the IT industry's annual attrition rate at 20% to 40%, but these reported values tend to be underestimated. My personal experience and the informal chats I have had with executives from many companies are consistent and reveal that this number could be under-reported due to different methods employed by different SPOs to report attrition. The best way for any SRO to manage attrition is to define targets for their SPOs based on the business they do.

Innovation Targets

Innovation involves SPOs proposing ideas to SROs that can bring value to the latter. This one of the hot topics discussed by nearly all customers in the IT industry today and is constantly referred to as *innovation*. Many customers are dissatisfied with their SPOs' focus on innovation, and many SPOs do not understand what their customers expect from them with respect to innovation.

Innovation is a broad term. Without defining it within the specific relationship between an SPO and SRO, it is difficult to manage expectations on both ends.

As discussed earlier, SROs need to ensure that they understand the full structure of their SPO. First, it is a good practice to understand the overall organizational structure and its entities, such as horizontals and their services, COEs and their expertise, the market intelligence function, and other such entities. Next, it is essential to mandate that SPOs keep SRO personnel updated on available services via whatever modes of communication (such as newsletters and seminars) are best-suited to the SRO. However, this in itself does not guarantee that the SRO can access the SPO's full innovation potential. The SRO needs to define an innovation target for the SPO, as explained in the following case study involving NDC Financials.

The SRO also needs to appoint an account champion or a consultative seller from the SPO who is responsible for driving innovations. This individual in the SPO has an overall view of the different practices and services in the organization. This person maps the SRO technology landscape and business to the SPO's services, keeps abreast of new services and advancements in the SPO, and identifies potential services that can bring value to the customer.

Client Profile: Leading financial services company in United States

Client name: NDC Financials

Size: 55,800 employees

Number of Service Providers: 3

NDC Financials is one of the largest financial services companies in the United States, providing investment-management and wealth-management services to its customers across the globe. The company has outsourced 70% of its IT business to three Tier-1 IT SPOs for services such as application development and maintenance, consulting, and business process outsourcing. As part of the innovation theme, NDC Financials, after consulting with a third-party consulting firm, has defined a framework mandating that all three SPOs bring new ideas in a systematic way and work with a selected set of people from the SRO such as technical architects, business architects, and project managers to validate the merits of each idea. NDC Financials mandates that each SPO identify an account champion who is responsible for presenting new ideas that can bring value to the SRO. Once a certain idea has been accepted, it is presented in the Innovation Board, which is composed of an executive team from both the SPO and NDC Financials. In this Board forum, ideas are discussed and selected for implementation. When an idea is selected for implementation, it is referred to as an *innovation*. NDC Financials has defined a target of receiving ten innovations from each SPO every year that can either provide cost benefits or improve existing business processes. This target is linked to a 2% performance bonus for each SPO. I have encountered several other cases in which financial bonuses and penalties were applied to innovation targets.

Although hard innovation targets are defined for the SPOs, the management of NDC Financials makes sure the company provides full support toward achievement of those innovation targets. This includes

- Creating a dedicated team to support the SPOs

- Ensuring that management maintains focus on supporting the SPOs, which is achieved with several feedback sessions

- Ensuring that ideas are validated at the right time

- Managing innovation as a collaborative agenda

- Mitigating challenges, risks, and issues on a priority basis

NDC Financials is a classic case study. It not only managed to extract the full potential of its SPOs but also supported the SPOs fully at each and every stage, thus enabling the parties to be together successful.

Pricing Models: Fixed Price vs. Time and Materials vs. Staff Augmentation

Different SROs follow different pricing models with their SPOs based on levels of trust, knowledge about what has to be achieved, comfort level, and many other factors. Each model has merits and demerits and should be carefully considered.

- *Fixed price:* With a fixed-price contract, a fixed fee is paid for performing a set of activities for a certain project scope. Activities could include creating design documents, developing software, and testing software. This type of contract is best for projects with well-defined requirements at the outset. The total cost of the project cannot exceed the established baseline, and fixed-price contracts tend to be less flexible with regard to managing changes. Any new requirements that arise during implementation and any changes in requirements may lead to price renegotiation and changes to the project's schedule, which can sometimes be disappointing to both the SPO and SRO.

- *Time and materials (T&M)*: With a T&M contract, the SRO pays for one or more resources in the form of an hourly or daily rate and can usually direct how that time is spent. The SPO and SRO agree up front about the deliverables to be produced for a given task. Sometimes there is also an SLA defined to address the quality of resources and deliverables.

- *Staff augmentation*: With a staff augmentation contract, one or more resources are sourced by the SPO for a fixed daily or hourly rate, and the SPO has no responsibility for managing those resources. Regardless of the workload, the SRO pays the SPO for the requested resources for the contracted period of time. Day-to-day management is done by employees of the SRO. This model is typically applied when the SRO knows that there will be a confirmed workload for all resources and wants to manage the resources itself. With this type of contract, the SPO has limited accountability for delivery.

Although many organizations tend to prefer fixed-price contracts, these contracts require a thorough understanding of how to estimate a fixed price for a project. Otherwise, a project can be overestimated, and the SRO may end up paying more than required. Alternatively, a project may be underestimated, which can result in an SPO experiencing a financial loss; this can lead to contentious debate and the termination of business relationships.

Selecting the best approach is based on the SRO's level of experience with each type of model (fixed price, T&M, and staff augmentation) and the kind of work performed by the SPO. A development project that has a fixed scope can be accomplished at a fixed price. A development project that has a partially fixed scope and a partially variable scope can be implemented with a combination of fixed price and T&M models. A development project that has a variable scope can be accomplished using a T&M model with an upper limit on cost, also called *T&M with a cap*.

A maintenance contract for which a fixed number of resources can be defined up front can be accomplished with a T&M model. A situation in which an SRO wants to have full control and accountability for project execution can be achieved with a staff-augmentation model.

Let's look at a case study in which NDC Financials incurred a major loss by following a T&M financial model for one of its maintenance projects. This is not to say that the T&M model, or even the staff-augmentation model, is not a reliable pricing model; but choosing the T&M model for its maintenance project did not prove beneficial to NDC Financials.

Client Profile: Leading financial services company in United States

Client name: NDC Financials

Size: 55,800 employees

Number of Service Providers: 3

NDC Financials signed a contract with one its Tier-1 IT SPOs to provide maintenance services. The contract was defined to source 20 full-time employees, of which 10 were supposed to be based out of the New York office and the other 10 in India. The contract specified that work packages would be allocated to the SPO staff and that an employee of the SPO who was the lead for this maintenance contract would estimate the work packages and come to an agreement on the estimates with NDC Financials. Once approved, the SPO staff would initiate delivery.

Because the contract was established with a predefined number of resources, contractually NDC Financials was supposed to provide work and pay the SPO for the complete 20-member team on a monthly basis.

The process worked well initially, but after a few months, challenges that had been previously hidden started to hit NDC Financials. A few of these challenges are as follows:

- NDC Financials was not able to provide work for the entire 20-member team on a continuous basis, but it still had to pay all members of the team.

- NDC Financials staff members responsible for this contract were under pressure to provide work for the full 20-member team.

- Because the contract was defined with a maximum of 20 members on the team, the team was not large enough during peak business times when additional work was to be delivered, which led to business user dissatisfaction.

The NDC Financials staff responsible for this contract came to realize that there was no reason for their company to take responsibility for this challenge and that it should be the SPO's responsibility to manage the resources. NDC Financials' only job should be to source work to their SPOs.

Year 1 passed with several challenges, but the SPO was sensitive and collaborative enough to help NDC Financials manage the situation. However, at the end of year 1, NDC Financials had to pay the SPO approximately $500,000 for idle time (periods when the SPO staff did not have any work assigned by NDC Financials).

In year 2, NDC Financials changed the contract to give more ownership to the SPO. It moved to a fixed-price model instead of a resource-based T&M model. Highlights of the new contract are as follows:

- *Fixed price*: The SPO estimates every work package before undertaking the work. NDC Financials must agree to the estimate before work begins.

- *Minimum team size of five people (one onsite and four in India)*: Regardless of the workload, NDC Financials pays for this team. NDC Financials is certain that at any point, there will be work for these five resources. This core team was created to ensure that project-related knowledge was retained.

- *Ramp-up*: New teams are to be in place with a 15-day notice in India and a 45-day notice at the other site. The SPO is accountable for making this happen. Based on the future workload, NDC Financials agrees to provide sufficient notice to the SPO.

- *Ramp-down*: Existing teams are to be ramped down with a 5-day notice in India and a 15-day notice at the other site. The SPO is accountable for making this happen.

- *Idle time*: No payment is made for idle time, and the SPO is to manage time to avoid such situations.

- *Resource bench*: The SPO is to create a pool of resources specifically for NDC Financials and within this pool, at any point of time, there should be 7% of resources who are available for the next assignments and are currently not utilized on any tasks. SPO to manage this resource bench based on current and future demand.

With this contract in place, in year 2 NDC Financials achieved 100% productivity from the SPO resources.

The takeaway message of this case study is that you should select the appropriate financial model based on the type of work to be done. This is one of the most essential elements necessary for an SRO to achieve maximum benefits from an SPO.

In-House Knowledge Retention

Knowledge management (KM) and knowledge retention are issues arising from the trend of broadening the scope of outsourcing in the IT industry. Each organization plays one of more roles in the value chain through strategic outsourcing arrangements. Such an arrangement is dynamic in nature: the level, scope, and role of outsourced activities are constantly shifting and have to be rearranged at periodic intervals to achieve the best from SPOs and the outsourcing strategy. This requires an organized KM process. With outsourcing entering a new era, where expectations are increasing each day for SPOs and IT outsourcing is growing in popularity, SROs need to be able to retain and create corporate knowledge and enhance their core capabilities, both in-house and for outsourced activities. Doing so mitigates the risk of vendor lock-in.

Business continuity knowledge retention (BCR) is the approach that should be followed by any organization that outsources all phases of a project to an SPO. This is required to ensure that technical and business knowledge is preserved with the employees of the SRO, which enables continuity of service with minimal effort even when the SPO contract is terminated. A team that consists of a mix of SPO resources and SRO resources is called an *assorted team*. Typically, the ideal assorted team has a ratio of approximately 20% SRO staff and 80% SPO staff over all phases of the project life cycle. Using an assorted team will ensure that BCR is successful and that knowledge remains within the SRO, to avoid potential vendor lock-in.

BCR testing is performed by an SRO to validate the success of BCR at periodic intervals ranging from every 2 years to every 5 years. During BCR testing, part of the SPO staff is asked to be absent from work for a specific period of time, and employees who are part of the assorted team are asked to manage the absent workers' IT business.

The following case study involves a leading bank in the United States that has been quite successful in effectively implementing BCR, which helped it to make a very strategic decision during vendor consolidation.

Client Profile: Leading bank in the United States

Client name: ABC Financials

Size: 200,000 employees

ABC Financials is one of the largest banks in the United States, with 70% of its IT business outsourced to three Tier-1 SPOs. Although outsourcing is strategic for ABC Financials, the company is always ready to face the worst market situations and prepared to manage continued business services. One area considered to be of the utmost importance as part of its outsourcing strategy is avoiding vendor lock-in, and BCR was applied very successfully in the organization across all vendors. Via the BCR model, ABC Financials mandated that its SPOs must have an assorted team consisting of a minimum of 25% overall staff from ABC Financials for every project and for every phase in the project life cycle. For example, a development project should have at least 25% resources from ABC Financials as part of the design team, development team, and testing team. The percentage on different teams can vary based on project types and phases, but the SPO should ensure that the overall ratio of the assorted team is maintained as per the agreement, with a minimum of one resource from ABC Financials deployed in each phase.

In addition to having an assorted team for ongoing and new projects, key roles such as technical architecture and business architecture are filled by ABC Financials staff.

At the end of every 2 years, BCR testing is conducted during non-core business days. *Black days* are declared for SPO staff, indicating that they cannot work on selected projects on those days. ABC Financials employees, who are part of the assorted team for the specific project, should complete the work as originally planned. Planning is done in advance, and project teams can request additional staff to complete deliveries. Additional staff provided to project teams are fresh resources, not part of the existing teams.

During BCR testing, 90% of all projects have passed their assessments. Analysis is performed on the remaining 10% of projects that fail, and appropriate action plans are defined.

With such an approach in place, when ABC Financials was planning for vendor consolidation, it was confident that there would be no risk to business continuity, even if the company reduced its SPOs. However, during the vendor-consolidation exercise, it was decided not to reduce the number of SPOs, but to add another level of checks on business continuity; business was interchanged between SPOs. For example, Company A was originally responsible for developing and maintaining applications for the corporate and credit card business units, and Company B was responsible for managing the savings account business unit. During vendor consolidation, Company A was asked to take over the savings account business from Company B, and Company B was asked to take over the corporate card IT business from Company A. Transition costs and other associated costs were to be absorbed by the SPOs, which ensured that ABC Financials was not financially impacted by this exercise.

This is an additional level of risk check that ABC Financials established in the outsourcing relationship. The approach gave the company confidence that it would not experience vendor lock-in with any of their its for any potential situation.

Pyramid Management

Another area of utmost importance is ensuring that an appropriate pyramid is in place that ultimately delivers quality service at a reasonable cost. Pyramid management entails ensuring that the correct number of appropriate employees with the desired skills and necessary experience are performing the proper jobs at any given point in time. Several studies have demonstrated that poor or weak pyramid structures can lead to project disasters due to subpar quality and missed deadlines impacting the SRO. In contrast, other studies have demonstrated a reduction in SPO profitability when a heavy pyramid is in place.

A typical pyramid is depicted in Figure 8-1: in this case, profitability is determined by an SPO, and expected quality can be determined by the SRO for a given project. Regardless of the type of contract, the pyramid is a key area requiring validation by the SRO.

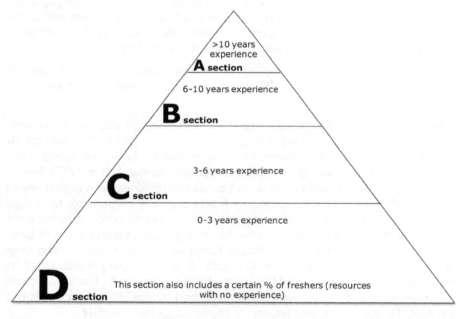

Figure 8-1. A typical pyramid for project execution consisting of resources with different experience levels

Section D consists of resources with fewer than 3 years of experience and typically also includes a percentage of recent college graduates. This is also called the *bottom* of the pyramid. These are typically junior developers and testers.

Section C consists of resources with mid-level experience (3 to 6 years), also known as *mediors*. These are typically developers and testers along with some junior designers, senior developers, and senior testers. This is also referred as the *bottom +1* of the pyramid.

Section B consists of highly experienced technical resources, including architects, senior designers, and sometimes senior developers. This section is typically referred to as the *top − 1* of the pyramid.

Typically, section A consists of project managers and, in some cases, enterprise and business architects, referred to as the *top* of the pyramid.

A pyramid for a project or a program consists of resources with different experience levels. Some SPOs maintain a lean pyramid and others establish a heavy pyramid, depending on the nature and complexity of the work.

A *lean pyramid* is one in which a large number of resources are deployed in the bottom and bottom + 1 portions, which results in a majority of less-experienced resources and a minimum of more-experienced resources.

A *heavy pyramid* is one in which the top and top − 1 portions are assigned more resources than the bottom, which results in few less-experienced resources and many more-experienced resources. However, with a heavy pyramid, you cannot assume that the team will deliver quality results. There should be a proper balance in the different sections of the pyramid to produce a quality deliverable, and this differs from project to project.

There is no rule of thumb to define an efficient pyramid; an SRO should learn to estimate the proper experience mix of resources to be deployed in projects. A lean pyramid can reduce the cost of a project (which can be determined if the SPO is transparent with you about the pyramid) but may deliver low-quality products because less-experienced resources are on the team. I have encountered several cases in which an organization deployed 80% freshers and the remaining 20% of the resources had experience ranging from 2 to 3 years. In some of these cases, the team delivered a very low-quality product. An optimal pyramid should be maintained for the success of any project.

In the case study with ABC Financials, the pyramid was made transparent between the SPO and ABC Financials for each contract type, based on which the price of every contract was fixed:

- A contract was created for development projects, with agreement on a certain pyramid structure.

- A separate contract was created for maintenance, with agreement on a different pyramid structure.

- Another pyramid was established for business analysis, contract, and consulting types of work.

- A fourth pyramid was designed for production support.

The pyramid structures were agreed on by both parties based on the complexity of the work and the business criticality of the applications.

For example, the pyramid for development projects under mainframe technology consists of 40% section D, with not more than 18% freshers; 30% section C; 20% section B; and 10% section A, which is the management overhead. This pyramid was mandated for overall outsourcing of development-type contracts with each SPO. In a quarterly steering committee, ABC Financials validated the existing pyramid against the agreed-on pyramid for each SPO, and deviations, if any, were discussed and agreed on. Each ABC Financials business-unit head reviewed the pyramid for their respective domain every month. Exceptions were discussed and mutually agreed on between the SPOs and ABC Financials.

This helped ABC Financials to ensure that the right set of experienced resources were deployed by their SPOs in projects and that the company was not overcharged by its SPOs.

Productivity

One of the most important areas to consider when evaluating software delivered by an SPO is productivity. Based on the type of project, productivity baselines need to be defined before the start of the project. For development and maintenance projects, where it is possible to count function points, productivity baselines can be defined based on productivity phases (specification, build, test, implement). There are several types of projects for which it is not possible to count function points, such as technical projects with no screens or functions and consulting projects with no software to be delivered; but even for such projects, you need to arrive at a productivity baseline.

In the case study with ABC Financials, when awarding contracts, the company always ensures that productivity baselines are agreed on with the SPOs. It is straightforward to establish a baseline for projects that can be counted with function points. For such projects, SPOs are asked to commit to the productivity baseline, and every project is measured against that baseline.

ABC Financials also ensures that a productivity baseline is defined for projects that cannot use function points. For example, an approach was defined to measure productivity for technical projects. This approach mandates that every project that cannot use function points must be deconstructed into small units, and each unit should be categorized as simple, medium, or complex. For each complexity category, a productivity baseline is agreed on with the SPO, specifying the total hours required to deliver each unit for each category. The baseline is compared against the in-house service that delivers similar projects, in order to validate the baseline's accuracy.

Although it is not a straightforward method, ABC Financials employed it to measure the productivity of its SPOs, and the approach was refined over time. Based on this method, ABC Financials defined productivity measures for each contract with its SPOs. SPOs were asked to provide productivity improvements year-on-year.

In my personal experience, fully utilizing SPO COEs provides productivity gains for organizations. It is essential for SROs to encourage their own and SPO teams to validate and adopt all applicable tools and techniques that are developed by COEs, to achieve productivity results. This is the true meaning of giving support to the SPO: the SRO works with the SPO to achieve the targets set for the SPO.

Key Points

- An SRO needs to understand the full structure of the SPO. This entails understanding the overall organizational structure and its entities and then focusing on those entities that closely relate to the SRO's business and IT landscape that can add value to its core business

- SROs should not try to squeeze effort estimates in an unrealistic manner.

- The SRO should focus on keeping SPO employees at the middle and bottom of the pyramid happy and motivated.

- SRO staff should communicate with SPO high performers continuously, regardless of their geography, to improve morale and motivation.

- Attrition, innovation, and productivity should be measured, and targets should be defined for SPOs.

- The three types of pricing models are fixed price, T&M, and staff augmentation.

- With a fixed-price contract, a fixed fee is paid for performing set of activities for a certain scope of the project.

- With a time and materials contract, the SRO pays for one or more resources in the form of an hourly or daily rate and can usually direct how that time is spent.

- With a staff-augmentation contract, one or more resources are sourced by the SPO for a fixed daily or hourly rate, and the SPO has no responsibility for managing those resources.

- SROs should retain and create knowledge in-house to mitigate the risks of vendor lock-in.

- SROs should ensure that an appropriate pyramid is in place so the SPO can deliver quality service at a reasonable cost.

Captive Center Management

Captive centers (or *captives*) are delivery centers owned and operated by SROs, typically in nondomestic, low-cost locations, that provide service resources directly to their organization. The personnel in a captive facility are legal employees of the organization and not of their SPOs.

Going back a few decades, most large-scale and Fortune 500 companies decided to establish captives, especially for their IT development needs. This allowed them to take advantage of low-cost labor and to be less dependent on their IT SPOs. However, this strategy has not proven beneficial for all organizations, and some of them have sold or shut down their captive units. Some examples of captive unit sell-offs well known in the industry were by Citigroup, Unilever, and Dell.[1] Research performed by Deutsche Bank on IT SPOs in the German market revealed that more than 60% of captive IT providers left the market between 2000 and 2006.[2]

---

[1]Stephanie Overby, "Offshoring: The Captive Center Rises Again," *CIO Magazine*, Jan 12, 2011, www.cio.com/article/2412141/outsourcing/offshoring--the-captive-center-rises-again.html

[2]"The Captives' End: Lebenszyklusmuster in der Entwicklung der deutschen IT-Outsourcing-Industrie," Deutsche Bank Research, February 2009, www.atkearney.com/strategic-it/ideas-insights/article/-/asset_publisher/LCcg0eS4t85g/content/the-case-for-captive-it/10192#sthash.jSZb6XA9.dpuf.

Nevertheless, wisely designed captive centers still exist. Other organizations, such as Motorola, GE and American Express,[3] have managed to derive benefits from their captive units while at the same time having part of their business still outsourced to SPOs. The captive model has advantages and disadvantages, and this model has proven beneficial for various organizations today because they have adopted the appropriate strategies to manage their captives.

There is speculation in the market related to the cost competitiveness of captive offshore centers, and many argue that the advantage of this strategy is fading. It is true that many low-cost delivery regions have seen significant shifts in inflation, leading to the perception that operating a company-owned IT or business-process center offshore is less financially beneficial. But most global in-house centers save a lot of money in addition to ensuring that critical work is kept in-house, knowledge is retained in-house, and the company has access to a broad talent pool. Cost advantage is not the only reason to establish captives.

Do You Need a Captive Center?

After the 2007–2008 recession in the IT market, the use of captives is again picking up. According to Jan Erik Aase, principal analyst with Forester Research, using captive centers has gained popularity due to the cost advantage it provides by moving work from developed countries to developing countries such as India.[4] However, as discussed earlier, although companies like Motorola, GE, and American Expressbecame instant success stories, many other captive centers faced issues during this timeframe.

There are several reasons why organizations establish captives, and one of them is to achieve a cost advantage by establishing the captive in a developing country. Other reasons are to protect intellectual property, bring IT innovations in-house without depending on SPOs for research and development labs, manage a consistent in-house delivery process to achieve predictable output, and manage SPOs' offshore staff via captives. This permit staff from headquarters to focus on the core business and reduce the risk of vendor lock-in with SPOs.

[3]Jan Erik Aase, "4 New Offshore Captive Center Models," CIO Magazine, July 27, 2011, www.cio.com/article/2405891/outsourcing/4-new-offshore-captive-center-models.html.
[4]Jan Erik Aase, "4 New Offshore Captive Center Models," CIO Magazine, July 27, 2011, www.cio.com/article/2405891/outsourcing/4-new-offshore-captive-center-models.html.

Managing a Captive Center

There are several types of captive models, but all seek to achieve the same benefits. As already discussed, some companies were not able to achieve the expected benefits from captive centers relative to the objectives stated before founding the captives. Several such failures occurred because the captives were mismanaged, with unrealistic expectations, and at the same time were given insufficient empowerment. Having the right strategy in place to manage captives is essential, and realistic expectations are of the utmost importance for a captive to be successful and to deliver results.

Clear Goals

The benefits to be achieved by a captive can be clearly articulated. It is also essential to define the goals for a captive to be successful, and the captive organization should be formed and governed based on those goals. Some captives are established to reduce the cost of research and development by shifting this work to the captives. Other organizations establish captives in countries where their IT SPOs are located, so that the captives' offshore staff can perform day-to-day vendor management. Some companies want to perform part of their critical application development in-house, so offshore captives are established. Other organizations seek to outsource their work to offshore SPOs and want their captives to manage these SPOs. Therefore these captives are established at a location nearer to their offshore SPOs. These are just some of the potential arrangements. The objectives for establishing a captive should determine the captive's organizational structure.

Let's look at a case study involving DEF Corporation, a multinational retail corporation that runs chains of large discount department and warehouse stores. Headquartered in the United States, the company has over 7,000 stores in approximately 17 countries.

Client Profile: Multinational retail corporation

Client name: DEF Corporation

Size: 250,000 employees

DEF Corporation had a market capitalization of $900 billion and IT expenditures of more than $800 million per year. This organization has engaged five large Tier-1 IT SPOs and four Tier-2 SPOs to manage its IT business, with 80% of the work outsourced to these IT SPOs. 20% of DEF Corporation's IT staff were managing the IT SPOs, including performing in-house development, which contributed approximately $200 million per year of internal IT costs. The business was growing twofold each year, and one of the goals of the CIO in 2008 was to bring cost and operational efficiency to the IT department, in addition to mitigating the risk of vendor lock-in with the existing SPOs.

DEF Corporation capably manages its IT SPOs and understands the dynamics of offshore IT business, due to its legacy experience in working with IT SPOs for almost 30 years. One of the strategies to achieve the goal specified to the CIO involved establishing a captive in India. The CIO was aware of the buzz in the market around several failures of captive centers and so translated the strategy into three initiatives that would enable the company to achieve its goal. The goal was to reduce cost, reduce dependence on local talent, and reduce dependence on external IT SPOs. The three initiatives were as follows:

- In-house and offshore development

- Vendor management

- Center of excellence

The initiatives were further broken down, and the company approached them as follows:

- *In-house and offshore development*: Development of non-core business applications to be performed in-house and from the captive. This division was named Corporate Technologies IDC.

- *Vendor management*: Delivery and vendor management for one Tier-2 SPO (Company A) to be fully performed by staff from the captive, which constitutes $20 million of IT spending on this SPO. This entails IT development and maintenance for two departments of DEF Corporation. This division was named Domain A and Domain B IDC.

- *Center of excellence*: Research and development for one business unit to be performed by the captive. This division was named R&D IDC.

With these three initiatives in mind, budgets were allocated and a captive was established in India. A consulting company was engaged to assist in setting up the captive.

Governance was defined with a CIO sourced from company headquarters leading the overall captive. Three unit heads were appointed locally: one to manage the development of non-core business applications, one for delivery and vendor management of Tier-2 SPOs, and a third for starting up the R&D wing. A new Branding division was established; it was lean but had the important responsibility of establishing the organization's name in the local region to attract local talent. A few other staff members from headquarters were made accountable for ensuring the success of this captive, and they were asked to operate from India.

The target was to reach a resource headcount of 50 in year 1. Local teams were recruited in all disciplines to start work for these divisions, and 20% of staff capacity was filled from headquarters in year 1. This team included 5% management staff; the rest were technical architects, lead developers and designers, and testers. The first 8 months of year 1 closed with several activities including recruitment, transferring knowledge to new resources, setting up the departments, and stabilizing the captive organization.

At the end of year 1:

- Corporate Technologies IDC delivered its first two projects successfully.

- The relationship between captive staff and Company A was established, and appropriate teams were in place.

- The R&D department was fully operational and delivered results after 8 months.

Looking back at the return on investment for year 1, the captive posted a loss, but this was expected; the CIO had made provisions for this in his P&L.

Year 2 delivered exceptional financial benefits, with almost 50% of the corporate technology projects delivered from IDC, 80% of R&D work executed from India, and delivery and vendor management for Company A performed by IDC for 50% of the projects. This led to a situation in which there was a need to reduce almost 100 resources from headquarters to achieve utilization targets of 80%.

At the end of year 3, a contract with one of the SPOs was cancelled. This work was moved to the captive center, which reduced costs by 30% in this specific business area.

This case study illustrates that for a captive to be successful, initiatives should follow goals, which should follow the specified strategy. Well-defined actions and proper investments can help to achieve superior benefits from the captive.

Empowerment

Empowered teams have increased levels of responsibility and authority over the work they are assigned to do, which ultimately leads to superior output. This empowerment gives them the autonomy to plan and manage work, make their own decisions, and solve their own problems—responsibilities that are traditionally owned by the team leader. Empowerment improves productivity.

As someone who leads a team, you are be used to being the decision-maker, problem-solver, planner, manager, and instructor. In short, you are normally the one who is in control. So, empowering others is no doubt very different from what you are used to doing. It means handing over much of this control, along with many associated responsibilities, to your team.

One of the reasons most captives fail is high attrition rates. Studies have revealed more than 30% attrition within captives, which is far higher than the average industry figure for IT SPOs. The results are low productivity, lost knowledge, and dwindling market brand.

One of the key reasons for such high attrition levels is a lack of employee empowerment. Even today, captives are considered back-office organizations, which indicates that low-profile work is performed by the captives and under the full supervision of resources from headquarters. Captives should be empowered similarly to headquarters, which leads to maximum output from the captives.

Figure 9-1 depicts the IT governance of DEF Corporation before its captive was established.

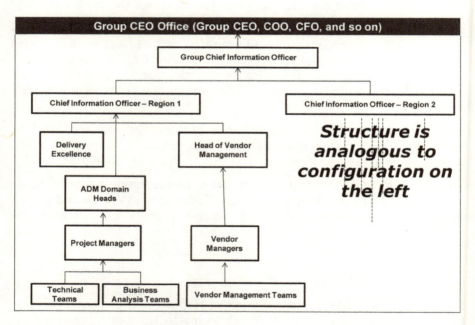

Figure 9-1. Governance of DEF Corporation before a captive was established

The senior management of DEF Corporation understood very well the cultural differences of varying regions, and the group CIO was aware of how to extract the best from his human resources. He knew that he would not be able to achieve the maximum benefits from his captive without empowering it as an equal to his other IT department.

Figures 9-2 and 9-3 depict the IT governance of DEF Corporation after the captive in India was established. A line in Figure 9-2 shows headquarter employees reporting to employees of the captive, and a line in Figure 9-3 shows employees belonging to the captive reporting to employees at headquarters. This is referred as *dual reporting lines*.

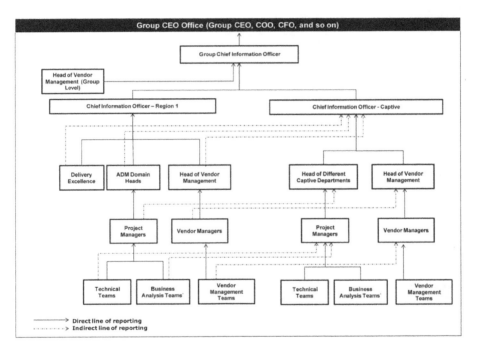

Figure 9-2. Governance (line of reporting) for DEF Corporation employees belonging to headquarters after the captive was established

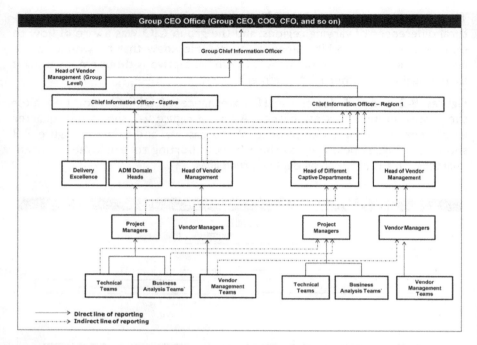

Figure 9-3. Governance (line of reporting) for DEF Corporation employees belonging to the captive, after the captive was established

The group CIO created a structure in which his captive CIO was as empowered as the existing regional CIO. All teams that could help make the captive CIO successful, and those that could contribute to the agenda to make the captive successful, were instructed to report to him along with the existing line of hierarchy, thereby creating a dual-reporting line of hierarchy at each level in the organization. The group CIO established a system in which yearly goals and objectives along with the year-end evaluation of employees were managed by both sets of supervisors in all applicable cases.

With this governance in place, all decisions were made with coordination between the captive and headquarters. This not only created a level of authority within the captive, but also empowered it by sharing the decisions and agenda of the captive with every individual. One side effect was that a few employees from headquarters were disappointed with this governance due to the dual line of reporting, but the group CIO knew how to manage these disappointments.

Empowering the captive with the proper level of authority is essential for establishing a successful captive. This can be achieved by defining efficient governance that equally empowers employees of all regions based on their line of control.

Human Resource Management

It is a well-known fact that when it comes to keeping people enthusiastic, money is surprisingly far down the list of effective motivators and stimulators of high performance. This becomes increasingly true as employees gain corporate responsibilities. This is good news not only for the nonprofit sector but also for profit-seeking organizations. It also implies that attrition is not always directly linked to money considerations.

Fat salaries and bonuses may improve employees' morale in the short term and may improve their quality of life outside of work, but it does not improve their quality of life at work. To keep employees loyal, committed, and performing to the best of their ability, you must ensure that they are kept engaged, empowered, and part of the organization. With captives being located remotely from headquarters, the personal relationship between staff across geographical regions generally is not as strong as between people in the same office. Some employees are skilled at networking and make efforts to establish relationships with other company employees, regardless of geography, but this group typically constitutes only about 10% of individuals. For example, the relationships among the staff of an SPO located at an onsite customer location are far stronger than those with employees located at offshore sites. This is one reason employees at offshore work sites may not come to the attention of their customers, even though they are high performers. Such a scenario is bound to exist in relationships between captive staff and staff located at headquarters. Often, such gaps cause relationship breakdowns, leading to low employee morale. This ultimately results in the attrition of even high-performing resources.

There are different ways to establish human resource relationships between staff from captives and headquarters. DEF Corporation understood that bridging the gaps between different regions was essential, and the company's focus was on bringing employees of diverse locations together. This can be enabled only by face-to-face interactions, which is one reason staff from headquarters were asked to temporarily relocate to the captive center during the initial stages of establishing the captive.

In addition, DEF Corporation made it mandatory for every member of the captive to spend their first 6 months working from headquarters, which facilitated relationships and interaction between peers. It was also mandated that middle management and senior management, including senior technical and business staff from headquarters, would visit and work from captives for a certain period each year. On every possible occasion, staff from headquarters, even at junior levels, traveled to the captive center.

These practices impacted the company's indirect costs but made its captive unit a coherent part of the organization. Each year, the captive improved its human resource principles to attract and retain talent. DEF Corporation experienced attrition that was lower than the industry average in its captive center, which ultimately led to a cost advantage

Vendor Management at Captives

The industry follows several captive models. In one such model, a captive center performs activities similar to the SPO and is geographically located at the same place. Work is allocated from headquarters either to the SPO or to the captive based on the complexity of the work, capability, and experience. This model has merits and demerits. It works well for software companies that need to manage huge workloads and do not want to depend fully on the SPO, to manage the risk of vendor lock-in. The side effect in this model is that the captive becomes a subcontractor to headquarters, similar to an SPO. This typically leads to less empowerment for the captive, because headquarters manages the captive staff on every task. This model has proven to decrease the benefits that can be achieved from captives, because resources ultimately feel less empowered, leading to high attrition. A superior model enables the effective and efficient work of the captive by allowing staff to determine the activities they want to perform, not in isolation, but in collaboration with headquarters. I refer to this as *empowerment*.

In the case study with DEF Corporation, the group CIO split the responsibilities between the captive and his IT department at headquarters in such a way that each geography had its own tasks to accomplish but both shared a common agenda of achieving the goals of the organization. I discussed that Corporate Technologies IDC is responsible for performing in-house development of its non-core business. The business head of IDC is empowered to make all decisions and to manage end-to-end delivery for all projects in this group, directly reporting to the CIO of the captive in India. He has a team of directly and indirectly reporting employees located both at headquarters and in India, which gives him complete control to autonomously manage the projects and human resources in his span of business.

Domain A and Domain B IDC reported to the India CIO, Domain A CIO, and Domain B CIO. Because the overall relationship and delivery of Company A (an SPO) was to be managed by Domain A and Domain B IDC, the head of this IDC was empowered with his own team of vendor-management and delivery staff to manage the relationship and delivery of Company A, directly reporting to him. Similar to Corporate Technologies IDC, he had a team of directly and indirectly reporting employees located both at headquarters and in India, which gave him the complete authority to manage the projects and human resources in his span of business. Vendor management for Company A was conducted entirely from India, with a dedicated vendor manager to manage Company A. This helped DEF Corporation move to India more work that Company A was performing, further reducing internal management costs. The head of this IDC, in consultation with the India CIO, Domain A CIO, and Domain B CIO, deployed part of his India team to headquarters to manage cultural and communication barriers.

For such a model to be successful, a well-defined communication approach must be in place. It must enable data flow and interaction between business users who are located at headquarters, the IT team located at headquarters, and the IT team located at captives. This complex set of relationships was well managed by DEF Corporation.

Bringing It All Together: The Power Captive Model

Similar to other organizations, DEF Corporation has experienced ups and downs while establishing its captive and running the captive's day-to-day operations. However, the leadership of DEF Corporation understood that their strategy was powerful and would generate results. I call the model that DEF Corporation used to manage its captive the *power captive model*. The company essentially brought together all the best practices and lessons learned during the course of managing its SPOs to establish and run its captive. Currently, this captive boasts approximately 6,500 employees performing IT business, and plans are to double this center as a result of the growth in DEF Corporation's core business.

A strategy must be a living, breathing document. As we all know, if there's one constant in business these days, it is change. Accordingly, your strategies must be adaptable and flexible so that they can respond to changes in both your internal and external environments. The CIO of DEF Corporation has constantly adapted his strategy based on the changing needs and challenges he faced while working with the captive center; this was one of the key reasons he was able to achieve the maximum benefit from the captive unit. Initiatives and direction were assessed for performance and strategic relevance every quarter. Strategy was annually subjected to full review to assess the benefits achieved and adapt to changing needs. Thanks to these practices, great leaps in growth and productivity were achieved.

Key Points

- Captive centers (or captives) are delivery centers owned and operated by SRO organizations, typically in a nondomestic, low-cost location, that provide service resources directly to their organization.

- Some examples of captive unit sell-offs well known in the industry were by American International Group (AIG), General Electric (GE), and Citigroup.

- Motorola, GE, and American Express are examples of companies that successfully established captives.

- The benefits to be achieved by a captive can be clearly articulated, but it is essential to define the goals for a captive to be successful. The captive organization should be formed and governed based on those goals.

- Captives should be empowered with decision-making capabilities similarly to headquarters, which leads to maximum output from the captives.

- Because captives are generally located remotely from headquarters, organizations need to enable frequent communication between staff across geographical regions. This creates team spirit and a sense of being one team, in addition to increasing the team's motivation.

- In a power captive model, teams from the captive are made part of the overall organization and are empowered to make decisions, and a higher level of collaboration and communication is enabled between different IT departments across geographies. In addition, captive staff and human resources are always kept motivated.

Exit-Plan Testing

The IT industry has gone through a major transformation in the past few decades. The idea that IT is not a strategically integrated part of business is old-fashioned, because almost all organization today recognize IT as the backbone of growing their core business. In parallel to this transformation, the term *service provider* became a lead offender. Here is a list of other phrases that industry members have changed in their vocabulary:

Partners rather than service providers

Partner technology capabilities rather than service offerings

Employees rather than outsiders/contractors

The latter terms describe thought processes from decades ago, whereas the former define what is expected by SPOs these days. Whichever terms are used, an SPO can be a partner to its SRO only when the SPO is bringing value that can enhance the SRO's business. Until then, an SPO is merely an SPO and is be regarded as a partner. Some SPOs have proven to be real partners, and they have achieved this label by considering their customers' business first, rather than focusing on their own business growth. If an idea can save several thousand dollars for the customer but at the same time decreases the SPO's revenue by a few hundred dollars, a partner will implements this idea, whereas an SPO will not even bring this idea to the SRO's notice.

However good an IT SPO is, it is essential for a SRO to understand that in the changing business world, there are no friends, and it is essential to be prepared for the worst. Exit management is an area that is not always given due attention by SROs.

Although it may not be obvious to focus on the end before even entering into an outsourcing agreement with a supplier, this is the best time to plan for the eventual termination or expiry of the agreement. This is called an *exit plan*. Although everyone wants to finalize the deal and establish good working relationships, it is essential for an SRO to ensure that a sound exit plan is defined and agreed on. Furthermore, it is essential to assess the completeness of the exit plan.

Exit Plan Focus Areas

Simply put, the exit plan and the exit-planning process are long-term, strategic approaches to the eventual transition of one SPO business to another. In the outsourcing context, this involves transferring business from one SPO to another or bringing work in-house.

There are typically three phases during an exit: the *before-exit phase*, *during-exit phase*, and *after-exit phase*. In the before-exit phase, a comprehensive assessment is performed to understand the different areas that require preparation to exit a SPO and are agreed on between the SRO and SPO. During exit is the phase when the exit is triggered as per the exit contract. After exit, necessary actions are taken to enable business as usual when a new party takes over the work.

You must consider several areas when defining an exit plan with an IT SPO, the key aspects of which are discussed next.

Scope and Duration

Agreeing on the scope of work that can be terminated and the duration required from the time the exit clause is enabled is essential. In most cases, the scope is the full contract's termination; but in some cases, only a fraction of the work can be terminated. An exit clause should be defined separately for each business domain in which the SPO is present and for each type of activity. For example, SPO 1 may be performing development and maintenance activity in the credit card domain and doing only maintenance in the mortgages domain. In this case, the exit plan's scope and duration should be defined separately for both domains, along with a clear agreement on the scope and duration for each activity, such as development and maintenance.

The duration can be determined based on the extent of outsourcing activities and the percentage of work that is outsourced.

Governance During the Exit Procedure

The governance required to make an exit procedure successful is another important area to plan in any outsourcing relationship. A governance structure should be predefined for exit, which determines the necessary management presence and checkpoints to ensure that the project is meeting the objectives of the specified exit plan within the agreed quality specifications, budget, and timeframe.

Documentation and Deliverables

Another area on which every SRO should focus while engaging an SPO is the documentation and deliverables to be produced by the SPO as part of its out-sourcing contract. Such considerations should be considered in detail. It can be argued that reducing the deliverables and the depth of documentation can reduce the cost of project development, but such a trick can end up putting the company at risk for vendor lock-in and can cause problems with the long-term manageability of the application. At the same time, requesting more than the required documentation and extensive deliverables makes the project and product development expensive. A proper balance should be maintained to agree on the deliverables that need to be produced as part of development and maintenance of any application, in addition to the number of deliverables to be produced. The goal is to ensure that at any given point in time, with the available deliverables and documentation, the SRO can take over work from the existing SPO or transfer work to another SPO.

Employee Transfer Clause

Even though a contract may be terminated with an SPO, sometimes the SRO needs to transfer employees from the exiting SPO to the SRO or to a new SPO to whom the contract is transferred, to ensure the continuity of work for the SRO. It is essential to define the terms and conditions of employee transfer. However, the final decision always lies with the specific resources that are being considered for transfer.

Investments by the Service Provider

One of the most debatable areas during exit involves costs. These consider-ations include the different types of costs or fees, when they will be payable, and whether they are factored into the agreed pricing model. All of these issues should be identified to avoid disputes and surprises at termination.

During an exit procedure in any for-profit organization, the party that is ending its contract will lack motivation to invest in the relationship. Similarly, an SRO will have the tendency to try to get the best out of the incumbent. An exit con-tract should clearly define the investments required from the SPO with respect to financials, human resources, hardware, and software during the exit.

Knowledge Transition

Defining the knowledge-transition procedure when an exit clause is triggered with the SPO is essential, because this procedure will determine the type of knowledge transition that is expected from the SPO in such a situation. This area determines how a transition is to be performed, the location where knowledge transition must be performed, and the acceptance criteria, based on which financial terms and payment conditions should be defined.

Shadowing

A knowledge-transition procedure determines the knowledge transition requirements, terms, and conditions. However, it is essential to understand that the new entity taking over from the incumbent SPO cannot perform its duties and continue service at the same level as the incumbent. *Shadowing* can help ensure that there is no disruption in existing services. This involves the incumbent provider offering guidance and reviewing the work of the new entity for a specified period of time.

Asset-Transfer Mechanism

During exit, the ownership and use of various assets, including intellectual property developed by the SPO during the course of the service provision, can be a contentious issue. Who should own intellectual property in development, and the scope of any relevant licenses, are matters for negotiation and should be agreed on up front.

As with assets, equipment, and contracts, it is important to identify which rights are to be the subject of ownership or license discussions. Suppliers often fail to record adequately what they have developed. This issue can be avoided through effective contract management during the course of the outsourcing contract: in particular, by defining and recording what has been created by your supplier during the course of service provision.

Cooperation

It is always essential to define the mechanisms related to cooperation terms between the SPO and SRO when exit is triggered on an SPO. Such considerations should be addressed before entering into a relationship. The terms and conditions should be phrased in the most explicit manner possible. These differ from contract to contract, but the key aspects that need to be included are as follows:

- Base services that must be provided by the incumbent SPO, and duration once exit is triggered

- Human resources that need to be available, along with location details

- Transition procedures

- Documentation to be delivered, and level of completeness before exiting

- Acceptance criteria

- Financial terms and conditions during exit

- Management focus required during exit

It is essential that the incumbent SPO give full cooperation when it is exiting the relationship; terms and conditions related to this should be contractually documented.

Exit-Plan Testing

IT outsourcing can be a complex transaction, and the different scenarios for exit can be difficult to document. However, predicting these challenges and complexities and their associated risks at the outset, and addressing them in the contract and through appropriate contract management, can mitigate the risk of a contentious and unmanageable exit from the outsourcing contract.

Many organizations believe they have adequately considered the possible scenarios during exit planning, but the success of an exit cannot be determined until it is triggered. In many cases, organizations face gaps once exit is triggered on an SPO. This makes it mandatory for any SRO to validate the completeness of its exit contract at periodic intervals, ranging from every 2 years to more than 5 years, based on the size and type of work, and the complexity and criticality of the applications maintained by the SPO. Enabling exit procedures every year can be expensive; the typical duration for a medium to large contract is every 2 years. It is also essential to agree with the SPO on the financial terms and conditions that will come into effect not only when an exit is triggered, but also during testing of the exit plan.

As discussed in Chapter 9, business continuity knowledge retention (BCR) testing is performed each year by an SRO to validate the success of business continuity planning. During BCR testing, part of the SPO staff is asked to be away from work for a specific period of time, and employees who are part of the assorted team are asked to manage the absent employees' IT business. Exit-plan testing goes a step further: not only is the knowledge of the in-house staff tested to see whether they can continue performing the day-to-day business without a specific SPO, but all other areas that constitute the exit plan are also validated.

The case study of ABC Financials provides a comprehensive view of how an exit procedure is enabled every 2 years with all of the company's SPOs to validate the completeness of the exit plan. Based on the exit-plan testing, gaps in the exit plans are identified and contracts are renegotiated with the SPOs. This is one of the reasons ABC Financials signs contracts with its SPOs for no longer than 2 years. The costs required to execute the exit-plan testing are shared between the SPOs and ABC Financials as part of the contract definition.

Every 2 years, at least 20% of the work performed by the SPOs is identified, and thorough exit-plan testing is conducted. A typical timeframe is during non-core business days when business transactions are minimal; those days are called *black days*. During this period, exit-plan testing is performed at the same pace as if the SPO was actually being exited.

Testing by Focus Area

Thought it is important to test the effectiveness of exit plan at regular intervals, it is not cost effective to perform the test on all areas covering the complete gamut of work that is outsourced to an SPO. Therefore, during exit plan testing, SRO needs to select samples in each area of work that is outsourced to an SPO and perform exit plan testing. This will give SRO a good view on the effectiveness of exit planning.

Scope and Duration

The scope of applications that will undergo the exit trial includes a combination of projects that are in development, projects that are completed, and projects that have not yet started, including projects such as maintenance and support. This selection is made to give ABC Financials a comprehensive view of the completeness of the sample data selected. It also includes samples from maintenance projects, support projects, and other types of work being executed by SPOs, including business process outsourcing (BPO). The scope is defined, and a duration of a few days is established for the exit trial for each SPO.

Governance During the Exit Procedure

As part of the exit-plan contract, the governance an SPO must deploy for the exit procedure is agreed on, and this is enforced during the exit trial. An exit manager leads the overall exit trial by each SPO, including a transition manager to ensure that knowledge transition is successful. Key team members are identified from the SPO to perform the knowledge transition. This team is called the *successor task force*.

Similar governance is identified from ABC Financials, led by an exit manager whose main task is to ensure that exit-plan testing is successful. In-house staff from ABC Financials who are part of the assorted team are responsible for planning the management of application continuity from the start date when exit-plan testing is triggered until after knowledge transition from the SPO staff has been completed. This team is called the *incumbent task force*.

Investments from the SPO

An exit contract defines the investments required by the SPO in case the exit clause is invoked on the SPO. The SPO requested a similar subset of investments in the exit plan to ensure that exit-plan testing will be successful. The subset of the investments is required in all areas in which exit-plan testing is conducted.

Documentation and Deliverables

The documentation and deliverables that were agreed on as part of the contract are reviewed for completeness by the successor task force, and these are used during the knowledge transition from the incumbent task force.

Employee Transfer Clause

Although there is no formal transfer of staff from the SPO during exit-plan testing, it was made mandatory by ABC Financials that the successor task force team identify individuals who are potential candidates for transfer in case exit was invoked on a specific SPO. There is no formal process to initiate this transfer, nor is there a discussion with the SPO. This exercise clarifies for ABC Financials the key SPO resources who are required to ensure continuity of services if the exit clause is enabled on a specific provider. The list of these resources is documented for future use, and after exit-plan testing is completed, these resources are called *key resources*. For ABC Financials, key resources are defined as 20% of the total resources from each SPO who ABC Financials thinks are essential for service continuity. Specific financial bonuses and penalties are assigned for attrition levels of these key resources over the duration of the contract with each SPO.

Knowledge Transition

In the knowledge-transition phase, the SPO staff must perform knowledge transition to the successor core team. In the case of ABC Financials, SPO staff are asked to perform a few days of knowledge transition on a sample application selected for exit-plan testing.

As per the exit-plan testing, plans are created with the SPO staff to perform knowledge transition based on the scope of applications selected for exit-plan testing. Deliverables and documentation defined in the exit plan are reviewed for completeness, and gaps are identified. Further, shadowing is performed by the SPO staff to validate the effectiveness of exit-plan testing, and assets and IPs are validated.

Case Study

The investments in exit-plan testing were determined to be important for ABC Financials, considering the size and criticality of the business they perform. After every exit-plan testing session, various gaps were identified, and new contracts were defined to correct these gaps. A few of the gaps are as follows:

- The governance agreed on with one SPO did not prove sufficient for making the exit plan successful.

- A successor task force that consisted of key designers and developers from one of the SPOs was unable to perform the knowledge transfer to the incumbent task force to the required extent for the maintenance stream. The incumbent task force was also unable to identify these gaps during the knowledge-transition phase, which led to a situation in which this task force was unable to develop new maintenance requests independently, even though the successor task force was shadowing them.

- Risks were identified in the use of several assets that were the intellectual property of one of the SPOs. The ownership of these intellectual properties obviously rested with the SPO. ABC Financials considered this a risk to its outsourcing business that might result in vendor lock-in.

- Another exit-plan test that failed involved BCR testing with one of the SPOs. The documentation and deliverables that were created as part of project execution were not sufficient for the incumbent task force to perform their exit-plan testing successfully.

After the exit-plan testing had been completed and gaps identified, an action plan was defined to close the gaps. The exit-plan testing exercise became a tool for ABC Financials to ensure that its dependency on SPOs was limited and that, whenever needed, the company could switch to in-house development or transfer existing work from one SPO to another, thus avoiding a vendor lock-in situation.

Key Points

- An exit plan and the exit-planning process are long-term, strategic approaches to the eventual transition of one SPO business to another.

- There are typically three phases for exit: the before-exit phase, during-exit phase, and after-exit phase.

- In the before-exit phase, a comprehensive assessment is performed to understand the different areas that require preparation to exit an SPO; these are agreed on between the SRO and SPO.

- In the during-exit phase, exit is triggered as per the exit contract.

- In the after-exit phase, necessary actions are taken to enable business as usual when the new party takes over the work.

- It is essential to agree on the scope of work that could be terminated and the duration required from the time the exit clause is enabled.

- The governance required to make an exit procedure successful is another important area to plan in any outsourcing relationship.

- While engaging an SPO, the SRO should ensure that documentation and deliverables produced by the SPO are comprehensive and adequate when an exit clause is initiated.

- Terms and conditions of employee transfer from SRO to SPO (or another SPO) should be defined. This is another key area of focus for an exit plan.

- Different types of costs or fees when an exit is triggered, and when they will be payable, should be factored in the pricing model when defining a contract with an SPO.

- The knowledge-transition procedure when an exit clause is triggered with the SPO should be defined up front.

- During exit, the ownership and use of assets, including the intellectual property developed by the SPO during the course of the service provision, can be a contentious issue. Who should own intellectual property in development, and the scope of any relevant licenses, are matters for negotiation and should be agreed on up front.

- It is essential to define the mechanisms related to cooperation terms between the SPO and SRO when exit is triggered on an SPO.

- Business continuity knowledge retention testing should be performed once a year by the SRO to validate the success of BCR.

- Exit-plan testing not only tests the knowledge of the in-house staff regarding whether they can continue performing the day-to-day business without a specific SPO, but also validates all other areas that constitute the exit plan.

Opting for a Single IT Service Provider

Over the past several decades, financial pressures and intense business competition have made business organizations and their IT departments rethink operational, employee, and financial resources by outsourcing part or all of their business processes to third-party SPOs. The percentage of outsourcing started small a few decades ago and has grown to more than 80% of all IT work being outsourced to SPOs. The more an organization outsources its IT work, the greater the management overhead of managing the SPOs (also called *vendors*). This arrangement can become complicated as an organization engages increasing numbers of SPOs for its IT business.

Almost all large organizations I have worked with since 2005 utilize multiple SPOs to manage their IT businesses. Each SPO is asked to manage the IT needs of one of multiple related business units from each SRO. Deciding on an SPO is in itself a complex task for an SRO, because it involves understanding the strengths and weaknesses of each SPO to achieve the desired results. With the increasing focus on computers to manage and increase business, IT spending across the globe is growing every day. To cope with this increase in IT spending and to manage the risk of vendor lock-in with existing SPOs, organizations are tending to engage increasing numbers of new SPOs to perform IT services by trying to equally distribute their IT work across these SPOs.

There are pros and cons involved in using multiple IT SPOs.

Pros:

- The risk of vendor lock-in with one SPO is reduced.

- SPOs can be selected and awarded contracts based on the strengths they carry in a specific area, which means an optimal choice of SPO can be made.

- Negotiations can be better handled with the multiple-SPO approach.

Cons:

- Vendor management overhead costs are increased.

- The SRO needs to understand the strengths and weaknesses of each of its SPOs, to extract the full potential from each of them.

- Consistent efficiency cannot be achieved, because different SPOs function differently.

- Handover from one SPO to another is always cumbersome, and managing inter-SPO issues requires significant effort from the SRO. This is true especially in cases in which one phase of a project (such as development) is outsourced to one SPO and another phase (such as testing) is outsourced to another SPO.

- It is always difficult to select the best SPO for a specific contract. This is especially complicated for SPOs of similar Tier classifications who compete with each other, because many SPOs demonstrate similar strengths.

The Single Service Provider Approach

The single-SPO approach, also referred to as the *sole provider approach*, is one of the outsourcing strategies that has generated interest among SROs due to the benefits it generates. This approach means an SRO engages only one SPO for all of its IT needs, so there is no competition for the SPO of the specific SRO.

Some of the benefits that can be achieved with the single-SPO approach are as follows:

- Reduced cost in comparison with the multiple SPO approach, because service costs decrease with an increased volume of work.

- Vendor-management overhead decreases with a reduction in SPOs.

- Understanding and managing one SPO delivers better results and requires less effort than understanding and managing multiple SPOs.

- Using a single SPO can simplify implementing a unified process or methodology in areas such as project management, development, and testing.

- SPOs own business risks and issues jointly with the SRO.

- Hardware and software costs are minimized.

At first glance, the single-provider approach appears promising. However, impacts on the SRO can be terrible if the proper SPO is not selected or the SRO is not sufficiently mature to manage the SPO. Assuming that an appropriate SPO is available, this approach can generate positive results if and only if the following are true:

- A very strong line of hierarchy is followed within the SRO. Decisions at each level should be strictly followed by subordinate staff.

- There is a high level of trust among staff working for the SRO.

- There is full transparency in the SRO at each level, and two-way communication is enabled. Two-way communication indicates that decisions at the top are cascaded immediately to the levels below, and vice versa.

- A flat organizational structure is maintained, even though it has a strong line of hierarchy. This permits each employee to reach any other employee when required.

- Employees on the SRO staff are experts and understand their business and IT applications fully. This helps in negotiating the best cost for a service.

- Those in the SRO are motivated to bring the best possible value to their organization by extracting the most from their SPO.

- Full confidentiality is maintained in the SRO at each level regarding data pertaining to the relationship with the SPO and its weaknesses.

- People in the SRO have excellent negotiation and communication skills.

- People in the SRO have superior human resource management skills.

The Single Service Provider: Focus Areas

Selecting a single SPO means you are handing IT control to your SPO, with the desire that this provider will help you to cut costs, unburden you of nearly all project or business process responsibilities, and be unfailingly reliable. The SPO to choose in this context is one that is financially stable and whose strengths match your business needs and IT goals. For example, an SRO whose goal is to be named a top innovative company in the next few years should not engage an SPO that does not think about bringing innovation to its clients or does not have a track record of being innovative during an existing relationship. Another example is an SRO whose goal is to invest in technology A. Such an organization should not engage an SPO that does have current strengths in technology A or does not plan to invest at an organizational level in this specific technology. A suitable SPO is one whose current strengths fully match the current and future needs of the SRO.

Once a matching SPO is identified, the focus areas that become of utmost importance to extract full value from the SPO are discussed in the following sections. It is mandatory that all of these considerations and related investments be agreed on and contracted before employing a single SPO.

Throughout the rest of this chapter, I use the following case study to explain each of the described concepts. SAR Group offers a broad range of services such as banking, insurance, brokerage, and investment banking services in the United States. It has a market capitalization of $1 billion and an IT budget of $80 million. This company has successfully operated using a single IT provider model and has secured several benefits from its SPO. The single SPO selected is one of the Tier 1 India pure players, with offices located across the world; I will refer to this pure player as Company P. The contract between SAR Group and Company P is defined for 5 years.

Volume-Based Cost of Services

In a multi-vendor environment, only part of the IT business is awarded to each SPO. Hence SPOs tend to charge a premium for their services, and overall costs are typically higher as compared to those in a single-SPO model.

In the case of a single-provider approach, the profits that SPOs make should be negotiated based on the volume of work: the cost of the service should be less than in the case of the multi-vendor operating model. SROs should negotiate the lowest cost based on the volume of work that is awarded to the SPO. Cost of services should be inversely proportional to volume.

In the case study of SAR Group, the organization divides its work into different work streams, such as development (which consists of design and development), testing, consulting, maintenance, and support. Based on past experience, SAR Group can accurately estimate the volume of work (in person days) that should be contracted to Company P each year in each work stream.

A blended rate was agreed on for each type of work, referred to as *work streams*, to be delivered along with an agreed-on pyramid and locale. The rates were negotiated to be 30% lower as compared to the model in which multiple vendors were involved.

Definition ***Blended rate*** is an hourly or daily rate for a resource that is applied consistently for performing a set of tasks regardless of experience level or location of the resource. A blended rate can also be defined for a service. In that case, it is an hourly or daily rate for each person-hour or person-day of work that involves a team of resources with a predefined pyramid of different skill sets and predefined locale to deliver a specified service. An example of a service is software development or testing.

For example, a blended rate was agreed on for testing work with Company P based on the following terms:

- *Pyramid*: Testing work should be performed with a pyramid of 40% section D resources and 0% freshers, 30% section C resources, 20% section B resources, and 10% section A resources. Please refer Chapter 8 for definition of pyramid and the different sections of a pyramid.

- *Locale*: Testing work should be performed with 80% offshore and 20% onsite resources for each testing project awarded to Company P. The 20% onsite should mandatorily have an onsite project manager.

$200 per person-day of work was the blended rate agreed on for the testing work based on these terms. A project estimated for 2,000 person-days costs SAR Group $40,000. This was a cost reduction of 30% for the average blended rate as compared with a multi-vendor environment.

Cost reduction was one of the reasons SAR Group sought to move to a single-sourcing model. The business case for Company P to reduce its normal rate is that it is being contracted to perform the full set of IT business for SAR Group.

A minimum-volume commitment was agreed on as part of this blended rate for each work stream. As per the contract, any work beyond the minimum volume entails a further discount on the blended rate, because this means Company P is being awarded more business than foreseen, and hence there should be an equal benefit to both SAR Group and Company P. Year-on-year reduction of the blended rate was requested by SAR Group based on the committed volume.

If SAR Group is unable to achieve the minimum-volume commitment it made, it is liable to pay a bonus to Company P. This ensures an equal level of owner-ship of the profitability of both organizations.

Using a single-provider approach, it becomes essential to identify all existing types of work streams and, based on each stream, to arrive at a blended rate.

Pyramid

A *pyramid* is a mix of resources with different experience levels working to accomplish a specific task. The pyramid's structure has a direct influence on the blended rate. One of the reasons to select a single-provider approach is to ensure less management overhead; hence it is essential to agree up front on the pyramid required for each work stream. The blended rate is also influ-enced by the pyramid structure, and hence it is of central importance to agree on the pyramid. Once a pyramid is established with the SPO, it must be fol-lowed consistently across all projects.

The development work stream was one of the streams identified by SAR Group: it consists of design and development phases. SAR Group split the development work stream further into two substreams. The first substream addresses the development of regular and business-as-usual projects. For this substream, a pyramid was agreed on with 40% from section D and a maximum of 10% freshers, 30% from section C, 20% from section E, and 10% from sec-tion A. A blended rate was agreed on for this substream.

A second substream was identified for projects that are considered techni-cally complex, and which from past experience are known to require a heavy pyramid. A pyramid with 20% section D with 0% freshers, 40% section C, 30% section B, and 10% section A is mandated. A separate blended rate was agreed for this substream.

Agreement on the pyramid structure is another key area of focus when employing a single-provider approach, to arrive at a blended rate.

Locale

Defining a blended rate is directly dependent on the locale. For distributed development, it is very important to agree up front on the percentage of the team that will be located onsite and offshore. This agreement becomes important when using the single-provider approach, because the terms and conditions need to be defined at the start to ensure a well-managed and smooth relationship between the SPO and the SRO.

In the case of SAR Group, for each work stream, the company defined the percentage of resources that need to be deployed onsite and offshore. For development projects, the design and build team was arranged to be 50% onsite, on average, for year 1. For testing, the blended rate was agreed on with a minimum of 40% onsite, on average, for year 1. The agreements related to onsite percentage were reduced year-on-year with the reduction in blended rates. This percentage is managed to ensure that Company P is as profitable as SAR Group, because there is a year-on-year reduction in the blended rate expected from SAR Group.

Innovation

When using a single-provider approach, an SRO is fully dependent on just one SPO to bring new ideas to improve the efficiencies of the company's IT landscape and core business. Thus it is mandatory to agree on an approach or methodology based on which the SPO introduces new ideas to the SRO. I call these ideas *innovations*. Furthermore, there is a need to measure the effectiveness of this approach with a financial target assigned to the SPO mandating that the SPO present new ideas in addition to performing its day-to-day duties. It is also essential that the SPO engage all applicable horizontals, COEs, and market intelligence divisions to generate new ideas.

In the case of SAR Group, the company mandates that the SPO propose a minimum of 20 new innovations per year that are applicable to SAR Group's business or IT landscape. The target is that at least 10 innovations should be implementable and should demonstrate tangible benefits for SAR Group. Every month, new innovations are validated with the senior IT management of SAR Group, and applicable ideas are selected for implementation. Various horizontals and COEs of Company P are engaged in this initiative. The success of innovation is determined based on the innovations selected for implementation each year. Failure to reach the target of 10 innovations per year imposes a penalty of 2% on the overall IT fees paid by SAR Group to Company P. The methodology defined for innovation by SAR Group is robust, with clear validation points. However, a detailed presentation of innovation analysis is outside the scope of this book.

Governance

It is essential when using a single-provider approach to define governance that enables the SRO to reach employees of the SPO who are senior in the hierarchy, to solve issues beyond the control of the teams interacting with the SRO on a day-to-day basis. The SRO should clearly understand the governance structure of the SPO and the key points of contact. The SRO needs to secure a commitment from the SPO's senior executives, such as the vertical CEO, that they will commit to the relationship and be available whenever necessary.

SAR Group mandates that the CEO of Company P should be present at the quarterly steering committee meetings to discuss strategic issues and to validate the relationship on an ongoing basis.

Productivity

Productivity is a measure based on which an SRO can determine the profitability it derives from its SPO. The blended rate is one measure, but without first establishing a baseline of productivity, benefits cannot be measured.

SAR Group ensured that a baseline was agreed on with Company P for each work stream that can be quantified by the function-point mechanism. The industry average was the selected baseline, with a year-on-year improvement in productivity of 2% that should be achieved by Company P for each work stream. For projects in which function-point counting cannot be performed, internal measurement criteria are defined, baselined, and tracked.

Assorted Team

A team that consists of a mix of SPO resources and SRO resources is called an *assorted team*. In-house knowledge retention is another important area of focus when outsourcing business to a third-party organization. This becomes much more important in a single-sourcing model, because there is a high probability of vendor lock-in if knowledge is not retained within the SRO. Having an assorted team is one of the strategies adopted by most organizations using a single-sourcing model, because it ensures that knowledge is retained in-house in each work stream with which the SPO is working.

When defining a contract with Company P, SAR Group mandated that a minimum of 30% of the staff from the IT department of SAR Group are made part of the team managed by Company P for each work stream. There can be exceptions in a few cases, not exceeding 5% of the overall outsourcing business. In these exceptional cases, it is contractually agreed that knowledge transition is assigned to identified members of SAR Group after work is completed by Company P. Documentation is key to avoid vendor lock-in, and for every segment of work performed by Company P, guidelines are defined concerning the level of detail required for each deliverable; these are reviewed and approved on a periodic basis by SAR Group.

Attrition and Core Teams

A single-provider relationship does not provide a chance for the SRO to seek alternate solutions beyond the current SPO that has been selected to perform the SRO's IT business. One area that concerns most organizations in an outsourcing relationship is human resource attrition in the SPO. A high attrition rate may result in lost knowledge and low productivity. Attrition targets should be defined for SPOs for teams deployed to deliver IT services, and these targets should be tracked and managed at periodic intervals. In a single-provider context, not only is it mandatory to define targets for attrition, but it is also essential to define a mechanism that motivates teams to continue working with the SRO.

SAR Group has defined a maximum attrition target of 12% for the entire team, because Company P revealed that its attrition at the company level is 12%. For the core team, SAR Group mandates a maximum attrition target of 5%, which is measured year-on-year. Attrition higher than these targets imposes a financial penalty on Company P, and targets are defined based on which Company P is mandated to take all steps to retain the resources. If attrition falls below the targets, SAR Group has agreed to pay a motivation bonus to all core teams from Company P, to ensure that the teams are motivated and attrition levels are minimal. The motivation bonus mandates Company P to reserve a fixed amount of money every year, and an equal amount is paid by SAR Group. At the end of every year in December, this money is distributed to all core team members.

Human Resource Management

In a single-provider context, regardless of whether the employees are from the SRO or are sourced from the SPO, human resource management needs to be performed consistently. The SRO must manage SPO teams in the same way as its own resources and keep them motivated. In some single-provider relationships, appraisals of SPO staff are performed jointly by supervisors from the SPO and SRO, to ensure that transparent feedback is given and individuals are recognized for their good work, and that their development needs are properly identified.

SAR Group ensures that, in addition to defining motivation bonuses for SPO staff, eligible individuals and teams are rewarded and recognized with various awards and benefits. This keeps team motivation high, thereby ensuring superior results and minimal attrition.

The Single Service Provider: Conclusions

Although there are benefits to selecting a single-SPO relationship, the consequences of a poorly managed relationship can be a major disaster to the SRO. This can lead to vendor lock-in, large-scale in-house staff attrition, business dissatisfaction, and, often, large impacts even on the core business. A single-SPO approach should be very carefully considered before implementation. It should be adopted by an organization that has a very strong track record of delivering projects in-house: this means the company's staff should be as strong as the SPO's staff when it comes to delivering projects, in addition to having a strong track record of managing SPOs. A capable SRO can achieve exceptional benefits in a single-SPO relationship and can obtain the best possible performance from its SPO.

Key Points

- The single-SPO approach involves an SRO engaging only one SPO for all of its IT needs. No competition is involved for the SPO for the specific SRO.

- In a single-provider approach, the profits that SPOs make should be negotiated based on the volume of work. The cost of service should typically be less than in the multi-vendor operating model.

- In a single-provider approach, it is important to agree on the pyramid that will be deployed by the SPO for each service.

- In a single-provider approach, it is important to agree on the locale that will be used by the SPO for each service.

- It is mandatory to agree on an approach or methodology based on which the SPO introduces new ideas to the SRO.

- It is essential when using a single-provider approach to define governance that enables the SRO to reach senior SPO employees to solve issues beyond the control of the teams interacting with the SRO on a day-to-day basis.

- A productivity baseline should be agreed on and should be measurable in a single-provider approach.

- A team that consists of a mix of SPO resources and SRO resources is called an assorted team.

- Using an assorted team with a single-sourcing model ensures that knowledge is retained in-house in each work stream with which the SPO is working.

- Attrition targets should be defined for SPOs for the teams deployed to deliver IT services. These targets should be tracked and managed at periodic intervals.

- The SRO needs to manage SPO teams the same as its own resources and keep them motivated.

I

Index

Get the eBook for only $10!

Now you can take the weightless companion with you anywhere, anytime. Your purchase of this book entitles you to 3 electronic versions for only $10.

This Apress title will prove so indispensible that you'll want to carry it with you everywhere, which is why we are offering the eBook in 3 formats for only $10 if you have already purchased the print book.

Convenient and fully searchable, the PDF version enables you to easily find and copy code—or perform examples by quickly toggling between instructions and   applications. The MOBI format is ideal for your Kindle, while the ePUB can be utilized on a variety of mobile devices.

Go to www.apress.com/promo/tendollars to purchase your companion eBook.

All Apress eBooks are subject to copyright. All rights are reserved by the Publisher, whether the whole or part of the material is concerned, specifically the rights of translation, reprinting, reuse of illustrations, recitation, broadcasting, reproduction on microfilms or in any other physical way, and transmission or information storage and retrieval, electronic adaptation, computer software, or by similar or dissimilar methodology now known or hereafter developed. Exempted from this legal reservation are brief excerpts in connection with reviews or scholarly analysis or material supplied specifically for the purpose of being entered and executed on a computer system, for exclusive use by the purchaser of the work. Duplication of this publication or parts thereof is permitted only under the provisions of the Copyright Law of the Publisher's location, in its current version, and permission for use must always be obtained from Springer. Permissions for use may be obtained through RightsLink at the Copyright Clearance Center. Violations are liable to prosecution under the respective Copyright Law.

Other Apress Titles You Will Find Useful

Offshoring IT
Blunden
978-1-5905-9396-7

**How to Secure Your
H-1B Visa**
Bach / Werner
978-1-4302-4728-9

Exporting
Delaney
978-1-4302-5791-2

**Software Projects
Secrets**
Stepanek
978-1-4302-5101-9

Metrics
Klubeck
978-1-4302-3726-6

The Employer Bill of Rights
Hyman
978-1-4302-4551-3

**Compensating Your
Employees Fairly**
Thomas
978-1-4302-5040-1

**How to Recruit and Hire
Great Software Engineers**
McCuller
978-1-4302-4917-7

**Smart and Gets Things
Done**
Spolsky
978-1-5905-9838-2

Available at www.apress.com

GPSR Compliance
The European Union's (EU) General Product Safety Regulation (GPSR) is a set
of rules that requires consumer products to be safe and our obligations to
ensure this.

If you have any concerns about our products, you can contact us on

ProductSafety@springernature.com

In case Publisher is established outside the EU, the EU authorized
representative is:

Springer Nature Customer Service Center GmbH
Europaplatz 3
69115 Heidelberg, Germany

www.ingramcontent.com/pod-product-compliance
Lightning Source LLC
Chambersburg PA
CBHW051244050326
40689CB00007B/1065